THE AUTHORS

Eddie Grieb has been the official statistician for SA Rugby since 2006, after similar appointments with the Far North Rugby Union in 1992 and the Griqualand West Rugby Union in 1999. Eddie has been involved with the *SA Rugby Annual* since 1999 and became co-editor in 2008. He has also worked for SuperSport over the past four seasons. He played flyhalf and fullback for Eastern Free State 'B' from 1987 to 1989 and flyhalf for Far North 'B' in 1991. Eddie lives in Pretoria with his wife Alida, and children, Lee and Edrich.

Stuart Farmer is one of the leading statisticians in world rugby. His company, SFMS Limited, is the official statisticians for Premier Rugby in England and the communications department of the Magners League tournament played in Ireland, Scotland and Wales. His test match rugby statistics archive is freely available at www.scrum.com. Stuart is the only external researcher used by UK broadcasters BSkyB in their coverage of worldwide rugby, and he has been the statistician at *Rugby World*, the best selling monthly rugby magazine, since 1997. Stuart lives in Leicestershire, England, with his wife Janet.

Dear Mark,
Happy 21st B-day!
Enjoy the 2011 World
cup! Love
The
Jnr
Bains
-x

THE SPRINGBOK HANDBOOK

EDDIE GRIEB & STUART FARMER

JONATHAN BALL PUBLISHERS
JOHANNESBURG & CAPE TOWN

First published in paperback in 2011 by
JONATHAN BALL PUBLISHERS (PTY) LTD
P O Box 33977
Jeppestown
2043

ISBN 978-1-86842-448-1

Cover design by MR Design, Cape Town
Springbok jerseys pre-2011 from private collection of Derek Roos
Springbok jersey 2011 by courtesy of SA Rugby
Typesetting and reproduction of text and picture section by
Triple M Design & Advertising, Johannesburg
Set in 8,75/10pt Sabon MT Std
Action Sketches by Richie Ryall
Printed and bound by CTP Books, Cape Town

— CONTENTS —

— FOREWORD —

The name Vula Maimuri might not ring any bells for most rugby fans, but it meant a lot to Eddie Grieb.

Maimuri, a Fijian forestry worker from Awanui, one of the northernmost clubs in New Zealand, was drafted into the Highlanders for the Super 12 in 2001.

And it was there, at Carisbrook in Dunedin, that Maimuri won his place in the record books, thanks to the keen memory of a rugby fan – and Eddie Grieb's dedication.

Early in the 2008 season Keegan Daniel scored an incredibly quick opening try for the Sharks against the Blues at the Absa Stadium. Newspaper reports variously noted that the try had been scored between 15 and 21 seconds after the opening whistle, but Eddie timed the tape himself and established that Daniel touched down in 16 seconds.

Thus Daniel went to the top of list as the scorer of the fastest try in Super Rugby history, displacing Chris Latham who had scored within 21 seconds for the Reds against the Brumbies in Brisbane.

But then, in this wonderful age of instant communication, an e-mail arrived from a New Zealander stating that there had been a quicker try, namely by Maimuri in a match in the 2001 season.

Instead of dismissing the claim, Eddie drove from Pretoria to SuperSport's studios in Randburg and drew the tape of the match – Highlanders vs Crusaders – from the archive to check for himself.

And there it was, confirmed by the match clock and Eddie's stopwatch. Maimuri scored in just 12 seconds, and has now duly been credited with the fastest try in the list of Super Rugby records.

Statisticians like Eddie, and his dedicated cohorts throughout the world, perform a vital task in rugby that is seldom acknowledged by the media, even though the scribes make constant use of their facts and figures. And thanks to the statisticians, players whose feats might otherwise go unnoticed and unrecorded, are given due credit.

With *The Springbok Handbook* Eddie has not only produced a fascinating record of Springbok rugby to be picked up and pored over, but has done a great service to the game. I know it will become a valuable reference in my collection of rugby books.

Dan Retief
SuperSport

— INTRODUCTION —

In *The Springbok Handbook*, Eddie Grieb and Stuart Farmer chronicle the history of South African test match rugby since that first match in 1891 until the Grand Slam tour of the United Kingdom and Ireland in November 2010 – some 395 matches in all. Their meticulous research has revealed even more interesting records and facts than have been unearthed before, and they also recount popular tales and folklore involving South Africa rugby over the intervening 120 years.

The more colourful characters amongst those who have been lucky enough to wear the famous Springbok jersey in combat, and a few who were unlucky not to, are brought to life with stories and anecdotes told and retold over the years.

All that, along with tables, notes and miscellany, makes the book a veritable treasure trove of everything you have possibly wanted to know about South African rugby, its players, its rich heritage, triumphs and tribulations.

— ACKNOWLEDGEMENTS —

We would like to thank a number of individuals who have aided immeasurably in the production of this book.

To Janet Farmer, Stuart's wife and business partner, for editing this edition.

To our friend Heinrich Schulze for his contributions, advice and the availability of his private library.

To Herman le Roux for his contributions as well as verifying information.

To Ashley Berry for his contributions, and for verifying information.

To Derek Roos for the use of the Springbok jerseys in his private collection.

To our wives (Alida and Janet) and Eddie's children (Lee and Edrich) for their love, understanding and diligence.

Finally to the top-class team at Jonathan Ball Publishers, including Jeremy Boraine and his colleague Francine Blum, for entrusting us with the project.

As with all books of this type, the odd omission and inaccuracy may appear. If any reader has any further information which may be of use, please contact the authors through the publishers.

Happy browsing …

— SOUTH AFRICA AT THE RUGBY WORLD CUPS —

South Africa did not take part in the first two Rugby World Cups in 1987 and 1991 due to the country's isolation from from virtually all sport as a result of its apartheid policies. In 1994 South Africa became a democracy after the first multi-racial elections and the country has competed in all the Rugby World Cups since then, winning the tournament in 1995 (in South Africa) and again in 2007 (in France).

— MOST TOURNAMENTS FOR SOUTH AFRICA —

Os du Randt and Joost van der Westhuizen are the only Springboks to represent South Africa at three different World Cups. Here is a list of players who have represented the Springboks at two or more tournaments:

No	Name	Years
3	Joost van der Westhuizen	1995, 1999, 2003
3	Os du Randt	1995, 1999, 2007
2	Mark Andrews	1995, 1999
2	Naka Drotské	1995, 1999
2	Ruben Kruger	1995, 1999
2	Krynauw Otto	1995, 1999
2	Chris Rossouw	1995, 1999
2	Brendan Venter	1995, 1999
2	Breyton Paulse	1999, 2003
2	Stefan Terblanche	1999, 2003
2	Schalk Burger	2003, 2007
2	Jaque Fourie	2003, 2007
2	Wayne Julies	1999, 2007
2	Victor Matfield	2003, 2007
2	Danie Rossouw	2003, 2007
2	Bob Skinstad	1999, 2007
2	John Smit	2003, 2007
2	Juan Smith	2003, 2007

No	Name	Years
2	Albert van den Berg	1999, 2007
2	Ashwin Willemse	2003, 2007

— MOST MATCHES FOR SOUTH AFRICA AT RUGBY WORLD CUPS —

Os du Randt, the only Springbok to play in the 1995 and 2007 winning teams, has played in the most matches for South Africa at Rugby World Cups. Here is a list of players who have played in ten or more matches:

No	Name	Years
16	Os du Randt	1995, 1999, 2007
15	Joost van der Westhuizen	1995, 1999, 2003
12	John Smit	2003, 2007
12	Percy Montgomery	1999, 2007
12	Bakkies Botha	2003, 2007
11	Juan Smith	2003, 2007
11	Victor Matfield	2003, 2007
10	Jaque Fourie	2003, 2007
10	Danie Rossouw	2003, 2007

— TEAM RECORDS FOR SOUTH AFRICA AT RUGBY WORLD CUPS —

Best performance		Winner: 1995 and 2007
Biggest win	66	vs Uruguay, 2003 (72–6)
Biggest defeat	20	vs New Zealand, 2003 (9–29)
Most points in a match	72	vs Uruguay, 2003 (72–6)
Most points conceded in a match	29	vs Scotland, 1999 (46–29)
	29	vs New Zealand, 2003 (9–29)
Most tries in a match	12	vs Uruguay, 2003 (12–0)

Most tries conceded in a match	3	vs New Zealand, 2003 (0–3)
	3	vs Tonga, 2007 (4–3)
Most conversions in a match	8	vs USA, 2007
Most penalty goals in a match	6	vs Australia, 1999
Most dropped goals in a match	5	vs England, 1999
Most points in a tournament	278	2007 (7 matches)
Most points conceded in a tournament	101	1999 (6 matches)
Most tries in a tournament	33	2007 (7 matches)
Most tries conceded in a tournament	9	2007 (7 matches)
Most conversions in a tournament	25	2007 (7 matches)
Most penalty goals in a tournament	21	2007 (7 matches)
Most dropped goals in a tournament	8	1999 (6 matches)

— INDIVIDUAL RECORDS FOR SOUTH AFRICA AT RUGBY WORLD CUPS —

Most points in a match	34	Jannie de Beer vs England, 1999
Most tries in a match	4	Chester Williams vs W Samoa, 1995
	4	Bryan Habana vs Samoa, 2007
Most conversions in a match	6	Jannie de Beer vs Spain, 1999
	6	Percy Montgomery vs USA, 2007
Most penalty goals in a match	6	Jannie de Beer vs Australia, 1999
Most dropped goals in a match	5	Jannie de Beer vs England, 1999
Most points in a tournament	105	Percy Montgomery, 2007 (7 matches)
Most tries in a tournament	8	Bryan Habana, 2007 (7 matches)
Most conversions in a tournament	22	Percy Montgomery, 2007 (7 matches)
Most penalty goals in a tournament	17	Percy Montgomery, 2007 (7 matches)
Most dropped goals in a tournament	6	Jannie de Beer, 1999 (5 matches)
Most appearances	16	Os du Randt (1995-2007)
Most points in a career	111	Percy Montgomery (12 matches)
Most tries in a career	8	Bryan Habana (7 matches)
Most conversions in a career	22	Percy Montgomery (12 matches)

Most penalty goals in a career	17	Percy Montgomery (12 matches)
Most dropped goals in a career	6	Jannie de Beer (5 matches)

— RUGBY WORLD CUP TEAM RECORDS —

Best performance		Australia – Winners in 1991 and 1999
		South Africa – Winners in 1995 and 2007
Biggest win	142	Australia vs Namibia, 2003 (142–0)
Biggest defeat	142	Namibia vs Australia, 2003 (0–142)
Most points in a match	145	New Zealand vs Japan, 1995 (145–17)
Most points conceded in a match	145	Japan vs New Zealand, 1995 (17–145)
Most tries in a match	22	Australia vs Namibia, 2003 (22–0)
Most tries conceded in a match	22	Namibia vs Australia, 2003 (0–22)
Most conversions in a match	20	New Zealand vs Japan, 1995
Most penalty goals in a match	8	Argentina vs Samoa, 1999
	8	Australia vs South Africa, 1999
	8	France vs Ireland, 1995
	8	Scotland vs Tonga, 1995
Most dropped goals in a match	5	South Africa vs England, 1999
Most points in a tournament	361	New Zealand in 2003 (7 matches)
Most points conceded in a tournament	310	Namibia in 2003 (4 matches)
Most tries in a tournament	52	New Zealand in 2003 (7 matches)
Most tries conceded in a tournament	47	Namibia in 2003 (4 matches)
Most conversions in a tournament	40	New Zealand in 2003 (7 matches)
Most penalty goals in a tournament	32	Argentina in 1999 (5 matches)
Most dropped goals in a tournament	8	South Africa in 1999 (6 matches)
	8	England in 2003 (7 matches)

— RUGBY WORLD CUP INDIVIDUAL RECORDS —

Most points in a match	45	Simon Culhane (New Zealand) vs Japan, 1995
Most tries in a match	6	Marc Ellis (New Zealand) vs Japan, 1995
Most conversions in a match	20	Simon Culhane (New Zealand) vs Japan, 1995
Most penalty goals in a match	8	Gonzalo Quesada (Argentina) vs Samoa, 1999
	8	Matt Burke (Australia) vs South Africa, 1999
	8	Thiery Lacroix (France) vs Ireland, 1995
	8	Gavin Hastings (Scotland) vs Tonga, 1995
Most dropped goals in a match	5	Jannie de Beer (South Africa) vs England, 1999
Most points in a tournament	126	Grant Fox (New Zealand) in 1987 (6 matches)
Most tries in a tournament	8	Jonah Lomu (New Zealand) in 1999 (6 matches)
	8	Bryan Habana (South Africa) in 2007 (7 matches)
Most conversions in a tournament	30	Grant Fox (New Zealand) in 1987 (6 matches)
Most penalty goals in a tournament	31	Gonzalo Quesada (Argentina) in 1999 (5 matches)
Most dropped goals in a tournament	8	Jonny Wilkinson (England) in 2003 (6 matches)
Most appearances	22	Jason Leonard (England) between 1991 and 2003
Most points in a career	249	Jonny Wilkinson (England) (15 matches)
Most tries in a career	15	Jonah Lomu (New Zealand) (11 matches)
Most conversions in a career	39	Gavin Hastings (Scotland) (13 matches)
Most penalty goals in a career	53	Jonny Wilkinson (England) (15 matches)
Most dropped goals in a career	13	Jonny Wilkinson (England) (15 matches)

— SOUTH AFRICA AT THE THIRD RUGBY WORLD CUP: SOUTH AFRICA 1995 —

Games and scorers:

Pool A

Date	Opps	Venue	Result	Scorers
25 May	Australia	Cape Town	W 27–18	Stransky, Hendriks. C: Stransky. P: Stransky (4). D: Stransky.
30 May	Romania	Cape Town	W 21–8	T: Richter (2). C: Johnson. P: Johnson (3).
3 June	Canada	Port Elizabeth	W 20–0	T: Richter (2). C: Stransky (2). P: Stransky (2).

RWC Pool A Table

Nation	P	W	D	L	PF	PA	TF	TA	PTS
South Africa	3	3	0	0	68	26	6	3	9
Australia	3	2	0	1	87	41	11	3	7
Canada	3	1	0	2	45	50	5	5	5
Romania	3	0	0	3	14	97	1	12	3

Quarter-final				
10 June	Samoa	Johannesburg	W 42–14	T: Williams (4), Andrews, Rossouw. C: Johnson (3). P: Johnson (2).

Semi-final				
17 June	France	Durban	W 19–15	T: Kruger. C: Stransky. P: Stransky (4).

Final				
24 June	New Zealand	Johannesburg	W 15–12*	P: Stransky (3). D. Stransky (2).

* After extra time.

Squad and Appearances

Coach: Kitch Christie. Manager: Morné du Plessis.
Captain: François Pienaar. Assistant Coach: Gysie Pienaar.

Player	AUS	ROM	CAN	SAM	FR	NZ	APP
André Joubert (Natal)	15	x	15	15	15	15	5
James Small (Natal)	14	14	–	x	14	14	4
Japie Mulder (Transvaal)	13	–	x	12	13	13	4
Hennie le Roux (Transvaal)	12	10	R	10	12	12	6
Pieter Hendriks (Transvaal)	11	11	11	–	–	–	3
Joel Stransky (WP)	10	R	10	–	10	10	5
Joost van der Westhuizen (N-Transvaal)	9	x	R	9	9	9	5
Rudolf Straeuli (Transvaal)	8	x	–	8	x	R	3
Ruben Kruger (N-Transvaal)	7	6	–	7	7	7	5
François Pienaar (Transvaal)	6c	–	6c	6c	6c	6c	5
Hannes Strydom (Transvaal)	5	–	5	–	5	5	4
Mark Andrews (Natal)	4	–	–	5	8	8	4
Balie Swart (Transvaal)	3	–	–	3	3	3	4
James Dalton (Transvaal)	2	x	2	–	–	–	2
Os du Randt (Free State)	1	x	x	1	1	1	4
Garry Pagel (WP)	R	1	1	–	x	R	4
Chris Rossouw (Transvaal)	x	2	x	2	2	2	4
Krynauw Otto (Blue Bulls)	x	5	R	R	–	–	3
Johan Roux (Transvaal)	x	9	9	x	R	x	3
Brendan Venter (Free State)	x	12	12	R	–	R	4
Gavin Johnson (Transvaal)	x	15	14	14	x	x	3
Christian Scholtz (Transvaal)	–	13	13	13	x	–	3
Adriaan Richter (N-Tvl)	–	8c	8	R	–	–	3
Robbie Brink (WP)	–	7	7	–	–	–	2
Kobus Wiese (Transvaal)	–	4	4	4	4	4	5
Marius Hurter (N-Tvl)	–	3	3	–	–	–	2
Chester Williams (WP) *	–	–	–	11	11	11	3
Naka Drotské (Free State) **	–	–	–	R	x	x	1

* Replaced Hendriks

** Replaced Dalton

Scoring:

Name	T	C	P	D	Pts
Joel Stransky	1	4	13	3	61
Gavin Johnson	–	4	5	–	23
Adriaan Richter	4	–	–	–	20
Chester Williams	4	–	–	–	20
Pieter Hendriks	1	–	–	–	5
Chris Rossouw	1	–	–	–	5
Mark Andrews	1	–	–	–	5
Ruben Kruger	1	–	–	–	5
TOTALS	**13**	**8**	**18**	**3**	**144**

— SOUTH AFRICA AT THE FOURTH RUGBY WORLD CUP: WALES 1999 —

Games and scorers:

Pool A

Date	Opps	Venue	Result	Scorers
3 October	Scotland	Edinburgh	W 46–29	T: A Venter, B Venter, Fleck, Le Roux, Kayser, Van der Westhuizen C: De Beer (5). P: De Beer (2)
10 October	Spain	Edinburgh	W 47–3	T: Vos (2), Swanepoel, Müller, Leonard, Skinstad. Pen. try. C: De Beer (6).
15 October	Uruguay	Glasgow	W 39–3	Van den Berg (2), Fleck, Van der Westhuizen, Kayser C: De Beer (4). P: De Beer (2).

RWC Pool A Table

Nation	P	W	D	L	PF	PA	TF	TA	PTS
South Africa	3	3	0	0	132	35	18	2	9

Nation	P	W	D	L	PF	PA	TF	TA	PTS
Scotland	3	2	0	1	120	58	15	6	7
Uruguay	3	1	0	2	42	97	4	11	5
Spain	3	0	0	3	18	122	0	18	3

Quarter-final				
24 October	England	Paris	W 44–21	T: Van der Westhuizen, Rossouw. C: De Beer (2). P: De Beer (5). D: De Beer (5).

Semi-final				
30 October	Australia	London	L 21–27*	P: De Beer (6). D: De Beer.

Third and Fourth Place Play-Off

4 November	New Zealand	Cardiff	W 22-18	T: Paulse. C: Honiball. P: Honiball. (3)D: Montgomery (2).

* After extra time.

Squad and Appearances

Coach: Nick Mallett. Manager: Arthrob Pietersen.
Captain: Joost van der Westhuizen.

Player	SCO	SPA	URG	ENG	AUS	NZ	APP
Percy Montgomery (WP)	15	x	15	15	15	15	5
Deon Kayser (KZN)	14	R	14	14	14	–	5
Robbie Fleck (WP)	13	–	13	13	13	13	5
Brendan Venter (Free State)	12	–	12	–	–	–	2
Pieter Rossouw (WP)	11	–	11	11	11	–	4
Jannie de Beer (Free State)	10	10	10	10	10	x	5
Joost van der Westhuizen (Blue Bulls)	9c	R	9c	9c	9c	9c	6
Bob Skinstad (WP)	8	R	8	8	8	–	5
André Venter (Free State)	7	–	7	7	7	7	5

Player	SCO	SPA	URG	ENG	AUS	NZ	APP
Johan Erasmus (Free State)	6	–	6	6	6	6	5
Mark Andrews (KZN)	5	x	5	5	5	5	5
Albert van den Berg (KZN)	4	–	R	R	R	R	5
Cobus Visagie (WP)	3	–	3	3	3	3	5
Naka Drotské (Free State)	2	R	2	2	2	2	6
Os du Randt (Free State)	1	R	1	1	1	1	5
Chris Rossouw (KZN)	x	2	x	x	x	R	2
Ollie le Roux (KZN)	R	1	R	R	R	R	5
Krynauw Otto (Blue Bulls)	R	5	4	4	4	4	6
André Vos (Lions)	R	8c	x	R	R	8	5
Werner Swanepoel (Lions)	x	9	x	x	x	R	2
Pieter Müller (KZN)	x	12	x	12	12	12	4
Breyton Paulse (WP)	R	15	–	–	–	14	3
Stefan Terblanche (KZN)	–	14	x	R	R	11	4
Wayne Julies (Boland)	–	13	–	–	–	x	1
Kaya Malotana (Border)	–	11	–	–	–	–	1
Anton Leonard (SWD)	–	7	–	–	–	–	1
Ruben Kruger (Blue Bulls)		–	6	–	–	–	R
Fritz van Heerden (WP)	–	4	–	–	–	–	1
Adrian Garvey (KZN)	–	3	–	–	–	–	1
Henry Honiball (KZN)	–	–	–	x	R	10	2

Scoring:

Name	T	C	P	D	Pts
Jannie de Beer	–	17	15	6	97
Joost van der Westhuizen	3	–	–	–	15

Name	T	C	P	D	Pts
Henry Honiball	–	1	3	–	11
Deon Kayser	2	–	–	–	10
Albert van den Berg	2	–	–	–	10
André Vos	2	–	–	–	10
Robbie Fleck	2	–	–	–	10
Percy Montgomery	–	–	–	2	6
André Venter	1	–	–	–	5
Brendan Venter	1	–	–	–	5
Ollie le Roux	1	–	–	–	5
Pieter Müller	1	–	–	–	5
Werner Swanepoel	1	–	–	–	5
Pieter Rossouw	1	–	–	–	5
Bob Skinstad	1	–	–	–	5
Breyton Paulse	1	–	–	–	5
Anton Leonard	1	–	–	–	5
Penalty try	**1**	**–**	**–**	**–**	**5**
TOTALS	21	18	18	8	219

— SOUTH AFRICA AT THE FIFTH RUGBY WORLD CUP: AUSTRALIA 2003 —

Games and scorers:

Pool C

Date	Opps	Venue	Result	Scorers
11 October	Uruguay	Perth	W 72–6	T: Van der Westhuizen (3), Botha (2), Van Niekerk, Delport, Fourie, Bands, Rossouw, Scholtz, Greeff. C: Koen (5), Hougaard.
18 October	England	Perth	L 6–25	P: Koen (2).
24 October	Georgia	Sydney	W 46–19	T: Rossouw (2), Hougaard, Van Niekerk, Fourie, Botha, Burger. C: Hougaard (4). P: Hougaard.
1 November	Samoa	Brisbane	W 60–10	T: Van Niekerk, Müller, Smith, Hougaard, Willemse, Fourie, Van der Westhuyzen, De Kock. C: Hougaard (5), Koen (2). P: Hougaard. D: Hougaard.

RWC Pool C Table

Nation	P	W	D	L	PF	PA	TF	TA	BP	PTS
England	4	4	0	0	255	47	34	2	3	19
South Africa	4	3	0	1	184	60	27	3	3	15
Samoa	4	2	0	2	138	117	18	14	2	10
Uruguay	4	1	0	3	56	155	6	39	0	4
Georgia	4	0	0	4	46	200	1	28	0	0

Quarter-final				
8 November	New Zealand	Melbourne	L 9–29	P: Hougaard (3).

Squad and Appearances

Coach: Rudolf Straeuli. Manager: Gideon Sam. Captain: Corné Krige. Assistant Coach: Rudy Joubert. Assistant Coach: Gert Smal.

Player	URU	ENG	GEO	SAM	NZ	APP
Werner Greeff (WP)	15	x	12	–	–	2
Ashwin Willemse (Lions)	14	14	–	14	14	4
Jaque Fourie (Lions)	13	–	13	R	R	4
De Wet Barry (WP)	12	12	–	12	12	4
Thinus Delport (Falcons)	11	11	–	11	11	4
Louis Koen (Lions)	10	10	x	R	R	4
Joost van der Westhuizen (BB)	9c	9	x	9	9	4
Juan Smith (Free State)	8	8	–	8	8	4
Danie Rossouw (BB)	7	x	7	R	7	4
Joe van Niekerk (Lions)	6	7	8	7	–	4
Victor Matfield (BB)	5	5	x	5	5	4
Bakkies Botha (BB)	4	4	4	4	4	5
Richard Bands (BB)	3	3	–	R	R	4
Danie Coetzee (BB)	2	2	–	R	R	4
Lawrence Sephaka (Lions)	1	R	1	–	–	3
John Smit (KZN)	R	R	2c	2	2	5
Derick Hougaard (BB)	R	R	10	10	10	5
Ricardo Loubscher (KZN)	R	–	15	–	–	2
Neil de Kock (WP)	R	x	9	R	R	4
Hendro Scholtz (FS)	R	–	6	–	–	2
Selborne Boome (WP)	R	x	5	–	R	3
Faan Rautenbach (WP)	R	–	3	3	3	4
Jaco van der Westhuyzen (BB)	–	15	–	15	15	3
Jorrie Müller (Lions)	–	13	R	13	13	4
Corné Krige (WP)	–	6c	–	6c	6c	3
Christo Bezuidenhout (Pumas)	–	1	x	1	1	3
Stefan Terblanche (KZN)	–	–	14	–	–	1
Breyton Paulse (WP)	–	–	11	–	–	1
Dale Santon (SWD)	–	–	R	–	–	1
Schalk Burger (WP)	–	–	R	R	R	3

Scoring:

Name	T	C	P	D	Pts
Derick Hougaard	2	10	5	1	48
Louis Koen	–	7	2	–	20
Jaque Fourie	3	–	–	–	15
Joost van der Westhuizen	3	–	–	–	15
Danie Rossouw	3	–	–	–	15
Joe van Niekerk	3	–	–	–	15
Bakkies Botha	3	–	–	–	15
Werner Greeff	1	–	–	–	5
Ashwin Willemse	1	–	–	–	5
Thinus Delport	1	–	–	–	5
Juan Smith	1	–	–	–	5
Richard Bands	1	–	–	–	5
Neil de Kock	1	–	–	–	5
Hendro Scholtz	1	–	–	–	5
Jaco van der Westhuyzen	1	–	–	–	5
Jorrie Müller	1	–	–	–	5
Schalk Burger	1	–	–	–	5
TOTALS	27	17	7	1	193

— SOUTH AFRICA AT THE SIXTH RUGBY WORLD CUP: FRANCE 2007 —

Games and scorers:

Pool A

Date	Opps	Venue	Result	Scorers
9 Sept	Samoa	Paris	W 59–7	T: Habana (4),Montgomery (2), Fourie, Pietersen. C: Montgomery (5). P: Montgomery (3).
14 Sept	England	Paris	W 36–0	T: Pietersen (2), Smith. C: Montgomery (3). P: Montgomery (4), Steyn.
22 Sept	Tonga	Lens	W 30–25	T: Pienaar (2), Smith, Skinstad. C: Pretorius, Montgomery. P: Steyn, Montgomery.
30 Sept	USA	Montpellier	W 64–15	T: Habana (2), Fourie (2), Smith, Steyn, Van der Linde, Du Preez, Burger. C: Montgomery (6), James. P: Montgomery, Steyn.

RWC Pool A Table

Nation	P	W	D	L	PF	PA	TF	TA	PTS
South Africa	4	4	0	0	189	47	24	6	19
England	4	3	0	1	108	88	11	7	14
Tonga	4	2	0	2	89	96	9	10	9
Samoa	4	1	0	3	69	143	5	15	5
USA	4	0	0	4	61	142	7	18	1

Quarter-final				
7 Oct	Fiji	Marseilles	W 37–20	T: Fourie, Smit, Pietersen, Smith, James. C: Montgomery (3). P: Steyn, Montgomery.

Semi-final				
14 Oct	Argentina	Paris	W 37–13	T: Habana (2), Du Preez, Rossouw. C: Montgomery (4). P: Montgomery (3).

Final				
20 Oct	England	Paris	W 15–6	P: Montgomery (4), Steyn.

Squad and Appearances

Coach: Jake White. Manager: Zola Yeye. Captain: John Smit. Assistant Coach: Allister Coetzee (backs). Assistant Coach: Gert Smal (forwards).

Player	SAM	ENG	TON	USA	FIJ	ARG	ENG	APP
Percy Montgomery (KZN)	15	15	R	15	15	15	15	7
JP Pietersen (KZN)	14	14	11	R	14	14	14	7
Jaque Fourie (Lions)	13	13	–	13	13	13	13	6
Jean de Villiers (WP)	12	–	–	–	–	–	–	1
Bryan Habana (Blue Bulls)	11	11	R	11	11	11	11	7
Butch James (KZN)	10	10	–	10	10	10	10	6
Fourie du Preez (BB)	9	9	–	9	9	9	9	6
Danie Rossouw (BB)	8	8	7	–	8	8	8	6
Juan Smith (Free State)	7	7	R	7	7	7	7	7
Schalk Burger (WP)	6	–	–	8	6	6	6	5
Victor Matfield (BB)	5	5	R	5	5	5	5	7
Bakkies Botha (BB)	4	4	4	R	4	4	4	7

Player	SAM	ENG	TON	USA	FIJ	ARG	ENG	APP
CJ van der Linde (FS)	3	R	3	R	–	3	3	6
John Smit (KZN)	2c	2c	R	2c	2c	2c	2c	7
Os du Randt (FS)	1	1	–	1	1	1	1	6
Bismarck du Plessis (KZN)	R	R	–	R	–	R	R	5
BJ Botha (KZN)	R	3	R	3	–	–	–	4
Johann Muller (KZN)	R	R	–	–	R	R	x	4
Wikus van Heerden (BB)	R	6	6	6	R	–	R	6
Enrico Januarie (Lions)	R	–	9	–	–	–	–	2
André Pretorius (Lions)	R	R	10	R	x	R	x	5
François Steyn (KZN)	R	12	R	12	12	12	12	7
Gurthrö Steenkamp (BB)	–	–	1	–	R	–	–	2
Bob Skinstad (KZN)	–	R	8c	R	–	R	–	4
Ruan Pienaar (KZN)	–	R	15	R	x	R	x	4
Wynand Olivier (BB)	–	R	13	–	x	R	x	3
Ashwin Willemse (Lions)	–	–	14	–	–	–	–	1
Wayne Julies (BB) *	–	–	12	–	–	–	–	1
Albert van den Berg (KZN)	–	–	5	4	–	–	–	2
Gary Botha (BB)	–	–	2	–	x	–	–	1
Akona Ndungane (BB)	–	–	–	14	–	–	–	1

Player	SAM	ENG	TON	USA	FIJ	ARG	ENG	APP
Jannie du Plessis (FS) **	–	–	–	–	3	R	x	2

* Julies replaced De Villiers.

** Du Plessis replaced BJ Botha.

Note: Bismarck and Jannie du Plessis are brothers.

Scoring:

Name	TC		P	v	Pts
Percy Montgomery	2	22	17	–	105
Bryan Habana	8	–	–	–	40
Juan Smith	4	–	–	–	20
Jaque Fourie	4	–	–	–	20
JP Pietersen	4	–	–	–	20
François Steyn	1	–	4	–	17
Fourie du Preez	2	–	–	–	10
Ruan Pienaar	2	–	–	–	10
Butch James	1	2	–	–	9
CJ van der Linde	1	–	–	–	5
John Smit	1	–	–	–	5
Bob Skinstad	1	–	–	–	5
Danie Rossouw	1	–	–	–	5
Schalk Burger	1	–	–	–	5
André Pretorius	–	1	–	–	2
Totals	33	25	21	–	278

— 2011 RUGBY WORLD CUP FIXTURES —

No	Date	Pool	Team A	Vs	Team B	Stadium	Venue
1	09/09/2011	A	New Zealand	vs	Tonga	Eden Park	Auckland
2	10/09/2011	B	Scotland	vs	Romania	Rugby Park Stadium	Invercargill
3	10/09/2011	D	Fiji	vs	Namibia	Rotorua International Stadium	Rotorua
4	10/09/2011	A	France	vs	Japan	North Harbour Stadium	Auckland
5	10/09/2011	B	Argentina	vs	England	Carisbrook	Dunedin
6	11/09/2011	C	Australia	vs	Italy	Eden Park	Auckland
7	11/09/2011	C	Ireland	vs	USA	Stadium Taranaki	New Plymouth
8	11/09/2011	D	**South Africa**	vs	Wales	Wellington Regional Stadium	Wellington
9	14/09/2011	D	Samoa	vs	Namibia	Rotorua International Stadium	Rotorua
10	14/09/2011	A	Tonga	vs	Canada	Northland Events Centre	Whangarei
11	14/09/2011	B	Scotland	vs	Georgia	Carisbrook	Dunedin
12	15/09/2011	C	Russia	vs	USA	Stadium Taranaki	New Plymouth
13	16/09/2011	A	New Zealand	vs	Japan	Waikato Stadium	Hamilton
14	17/09/2011	B	Argentina	vs	Romania	Rugby Park Stadium	Invercargill
15	17/09/2011	D	**South Africa**	vs	Fiji	Wellington Regional Stadium	Wellington
16	17/09/2011	C	Australia	vs	Ireland	Eden Park	Auckland
17	18/09/2011	D	Wales	vs	Samoa	Waikato Stadium	Hamilton
18	18/09/2011	B	England	vs	Georgia	Carisbrook	Dunedin
19	18/09/2011	A	France	vs	Canada	McLean Park	Napier
20	20/09/2011	C	Italy	vs	Russia	Trafalgar Park	Nelson
21	21/09/2011	A	Tonga	vs	Japan	Northland Events Centre	Whangarei
22	22/09/2011	D	**South Africa**	vs	Namibia	North Harbour Stadium	Auckland
23	23/09/2011	C	Australia	vs	USA	Wellington Regional Stadium	Wellington
24	24/09/2011	B	England	vs	Romania	Carisbrook	Dunedin

25	24/09/2011	A	New Zealand	vs	France	Eden Park	Auckland
26	25/09/2011	D	Fiji	vs	Samoa	Eden Park	Auckland
27	25/09/2011	C	Ireland	vs	Russia	Rotorua International Stadium	Rotorua
28	25/09/2011	B	Argentina	vs	Scotland	Wellington Regional Stadium	Wellington
29	26/09/2011	D	Wales	vs	Namibia	Stadium Taranaki	New Plymouth
30	27/09/2011	A	Canada	vs	Japan	McLean Park	Napier
31	27/09/2011	C	Italy	vs	USA	Trafalgar Park	Nelson
32	28/09/2011	B	Georgia	vs	Romania	Arena Manawatu	Palmerston North
33	30/09/2011	D	**South Africa**	vs	Samoa	North Harbour Stadium	Auckland
34	01/10/2011	C	Australia	vs	Russia	Trafalgar Park	Nelson
35	01/10/2011	A	France	vs	Tonga	Wellington Regional Stadium	Wellington
36	01/10/2011	B	England	vs	Scotland	Eden Park	Auckland
37	02/10/2011	B	Argentina	vs	Georgia	Arena Manawatu	Palmerston North
38	02/10/2011	A	New Zealand	vs	Canada	Wellington Regional Stadium	Wellington
39	02/10/2011	D	Wales	vs	Fiji	Waikato Stadium	Hamilton
40	02/10/2011	C	Ireland	vs	Italy	Otago Stadium	Dunedin
41	08/10/2011	QF 1	W C	vs	RU D	Wellington Regional Stadium	Wellington
42	08/10/2011	QF 2	W B	vs	RU A	Eden Park	Auckland
43	09/10/2011	QF 3	W D	vs	RU C	Wellington Regional Stadium	Wellington
44	09/10/2011	QF 4	W A	vs	RU B	Eden Park	Auckland
45	15/10/2011	SF 1	W QF 1	vs	W QF 2	Eden Park	Auckland
46	16/10/2011	SF 2	W QF 3	vs	W QF 4	Eden Park	Auckland
47	21/10/2011		L SF 1	vs	L SF 2	Eden Park	Auckland
48	23/10/2011		W SF 1	vs	W SF 2	Eden Park	Auckland

— WILLIAM WEBB ELLIS TROPHY —

The William Webb Ellis Trophy is the prize presented to the winners of the Rugby World Cup. The Cup itself was made in 1906 by Garrards jewellers in London and was subsequently chosen as an appropriate trophy for use in the World Cup competition. The word 'International Rugby Board' and, below, 'William Webb Ellis Cup' are engraved on the face of the trophy. The cup, which is often referred to simply as the Rugby World Cup, stands at 38 centimetres and is silver gilded in gold. It is supported by two cast scroll handles, one having the head of a satyr and the other the head of a nymph.

World Cup winners:

1987	New Zealand
1991	Australia
1995	South Africa
1999	Australia
2003	England
2007	South Africa

— WORLD CUP WINNERS' MEDALS —

Os du Randt is one of only five players to have received two winners' medals at different World Cups. The others are John Eales, Tim Horan, Jason Little and Phil Kearns, all of Australia for winning in 1991 and 1999. Kearns did not play in the 1999 final but received a medal as part of the squad. Eddie Jones, the 2003 Australian winning coach, also received a winners' medal in 2007 as Assistant Coach of the Springboks.

— YOUNGEST WORLD CUP WINNER —

Francois Steyn became the youngest recipient of a RWC winners' medal in 2007. Steyn, born on 14 May 1987, was 20 years and 159 days old on 20 October 2007 when South Africa beat England to win the 2007 RWC Final. Australia's Jason Little had previously held the record: he was born on 18 May 1970, and was 21 years and 68 days old when Australia beat England on 6 November 1991 at Twickenham. JP Pietersen is now the third youngest World Cup winner, aged 21 years and 100 days in 2007.

— ALPHABETICAL LIST OF SOUTH AFRICAN PLAYERS AT THE RUGBY WORLD CUP —

Surname, Initials (Name)	Province	Years	M	T	C	P	D	TP
Andrews, MG (Mark)	Natal	1995, 1999	9	1	0	0	0	5
Bands, RE (Richard)	Blue Bulls	2003	4	1	0	0	0	5
Barry, D (De Wet)	Western Province	2003	4	0	0	0	0	0
Bezuidenhout, CJ (Christo)	Pumas	2003	3	0	0	0	0	0
Boome, CS (Selborne)	Western Province	2003	3	0	0	0	0	0
Botha, BJ (BJ)	Natal	2007	4	0	0	0	0	0
Botha, G van G (Gary)	Blue Bulls	2007	1	0	0	0	0	0
Botha, JP (Bakkies)	Blue Bulls	2003, 2007	12	3	0	0	0	15
Brink, RA (Robbie)	Western Province	1995	2	0	0	0	0	0
Burger, SWP (Schalk)	Western Province	2003, 2007	8	2	0	0	0	10
Coetzee, D (Danie)	Blue Bulls	2003	4	0	0	0	0	0
Dalton, J (James)	Lions	1995	2	0	0	0	0	0
De Beer, JH (Jannie)	Free State	1999	5	0	17	15	6	97
De Kock, NA (Neil)	Western Province	2003	4	1	0	0	0	5
De Villiers, J (Jean)	Western Province	2007	1	0	0	0	0	0
Delport, GM (Thinus)	Falcons	2003	4	1	0	0	0	5
Drotské, AE (Naka)	Free State	1995, 1999	7	0	0	0	0	0
Du Plessis, BW (Bismarck)	Natal	2007	5	0	0	0	0	0
Du Plessis, JN (Jannie)	Free State	2007	2	0	0	0	0	0
Du Preez, PF (Fourie)	Blue Bulls	2007	6	2	0	0	0	10

Surname, Initials (Name)	Province	Years	M	T	C	P	D	TP
Du Randt, JP (Os)	Free State	1995, 1999, 2007	16	0	0	0	0	0
Erasmus, J (Rassie)	Lions	1999	5	0	0	0	0	0
Fleck, RF (Robbie)	Western Province	1999	5	2	0	0	0	10
Fourie, J (Jaque)	Lions	2003, 2007	10	7	0	0	0	35
Garvey, AC (Adrian)	Natal	1999	1	0	0	0	0	0
Greeff, WW (Werner)	Western Province	2003	2	1	0	0	0	5
Habana, BG (Bryan)	Blue Bulls	2007	7	8	0	0	0	40
Hendriks, P (Pieter)	Lions	1995	3	1	0	0	0	5
Honiball, HW (Henry)	Natal	1999	2	0	1	3	0	11
Hougaard, DJ (Derick)	Blue Bulls	2003	5	2	10	5	1	48
Hurter, MH (Marius)	Blue Bulls	1995	2	0	0	0	0	0
James, AD (Butch)	Natal	2007	6	1	2	0	0	9
Januarie, ER (Ricky)	Lions	2007	2	0	0	0	0	0
Johnson, GK (Gavin)	Lions	1995	3	0	4	5	0	23
Joubert, AJ (André)	Natal	1995	5	0	0	0	0	0
Julies, W (Wayne)	Boland/ Blue Bulls	1999, 2007	2	0	0	0	0	0
Kayser, DJ (Deon)	Eastern Province	1999	5	2	0	0	0	10
Koen, LJ (Louis)	Lions	2003	4	0	7	2	0	20
Krige, CPJ (Corné)	Western Province	2003	3	0	0	0	0	0
Kruger, RJ (Ruben)	Blue Bulls	1995, 1999	7	1	0	0	0	5
Le Roux, A-H (Ollie)	Natal	1999	6	1	0	0	0	5
Le Roux, HP (Hennie)	Lions	1995	6	0	0	0	0	0
Leonard, A (Anton)	SWD	1999	1	1	0	0	0	5

Surname, Initials (Name)	Province	Years	M	T	C	P	D	TP
Loubscher, RIP (Ricardo)	Natal	2003	2	0	0	0	0	0
Malotana, K (Kaya)	Border	1999	1	0	0	0	0	0
Matfield, V (Victor)	Blue Bulls	2003, 2007	11	0	0	0	0	0
Montgomery, PC (Percy)	WP/ Natal	1999, 2007	12	2	22	17	2	111
Mulder, JC (Japie)	Lions	1995	4	0	0	0	0	0
Muller, GJ (Johann)	Natal	2007	4	0	0	0	0	0
Müller, GP (Jorrie)	Lions	2003	4	1	0	0	0	5
Müller, PG (Pieter)	Natal	1999	4	1	0	0	0	5
Ndungane, AZ (Akona)	Blue Bulls	2007	1	0	0	0	0	0
Olivier, W (Wynand)	Blue Bulls	2007	3	0	0	0	0	0
Otto, K (Krynauw)	Blue Bulls	1995, 1999	9	0	0	0	0	0
Pagel, GL (Garry)	Western Province	1995	4	0	0	0	0	0
Paulse, BJ (Breyton)	Western Province	1999, 2003	4	1	0	0	0	5
Pienaar, JF (François)	Lions	1995	5	0	0	0	0	0
Pienaar, R (Ruan)	Natal	2007	4	2	0	0	0	10
Pietersen, JP (JP)	Natal	2007	7	4	0	0	0	20
Pretorius, AS (André)	Lions	2007	5	0	1	0	0	2
Rautenbach, SJ (Faan)	Western Province	2003	4	0	0	0	0	0
Richter, AJ (Adriaan)	Blue Bulls	1995	3	4	0	0	0	20
Rossouw, C le C (Chris)	Lions	1995, 1999	6	1	0	0	0	5
Rossouw, DJ (Danie)	Blue Bulls	2003, 2007	10	4	0	0	0	20
Rossouw, PWG (Pieter)	Western Province	1999	4	1	0	0	0	5
Roux, JP (Johan)	Lions	1995	3	0	0	0	0	0

Surname, Initials (Name)	Province	Years	M	T	C	P	D	TP
Santon, D (Dale)	SWD	2003	1	0	0	0	0	0
Scholtz, CP (Christiaan)	Lions	1995	3	0	0	0	0	0
Scholtz, H (Hendro)	Free State	2003	2	1	0	0	0	5
Sephaka, LD (Lawrence)	Lions	2003	3	0	0	0	0	0
Skinstad, RB (Bob)	WP/ Natal	1999, 2007	9	2	0	0	0	10
Small, JT (James)	Natal	1995	4	0	0	0	0	0
Smit, JW (John)	Natal	2003, 2007	12	1	0	0	0	5
Smith, JH (Juan)	Free State	2003, 2007	11	5	0	0	0	25
Steenkamp, GG (Gurthrö)	Blue Bulls	2007	2	0	0	0	0	0
Steyn, FPL (Francois)	Natal	2007	7	1	0	4	0	17
Straeuli, RAW (Rudolf)	Lions	1995	3	0	0	0	0	0
Stransky, JT (Joel)	Western Province	1995	5	1	4	13	3	61
Strydom, JJ (Hannes)	Lions	1995	4	0	0	0	0	0
Swanepoel, W (Werner)	Lions	1999	2	1	0	0	0	5
Swart, IS de V (Balie)	Lions	1995	4	0	0	0	0	0
Terblanche, CS (Stefan)	Natal	1999, 2003	5	0	0	0	0	0
Van den Berg, PA (Albert)	Griquas/ Natal	1999, 2007	7	2	0	0	0	10
Van der Linde, CJ (CJ)	Free State	2007	6	1	0	0	0	5
Van der Westhuizen, JH (Joost)	Blue Bulls	1995, 1999, 03	15	6	0	0	0	30
Van der Westhuyzen, JNB (Jaco)	Blue Bulls	2003	3	1	0	0	0	5

Surname, Initials (Name)	Province	Years	M	T	C	P	D	TP
Van Heerden, JL (Wikus)	Blue Bulls	2007	6	0	0	0	0	0
Van Heerden, FJ (Fritz)	Western Province	1999	1	0	0	0	0	0
Van Niekerk, JC (Joe)	Lions	2003	4	3	0	0	0	15
Venter, AG (André)	Free State	1999	5	1	0	0	0	5
Venter, B (Brendan)	Free State	1995, 1999	6	1	0	0	0	5
Visagie, IJ (Cobus)	Western Province	1999	5	0	0	0	0	0
Vos, AN (André)	Lions	1999	5	2	0	0	0	10
Wiese, JJ (Kobus)	Lions	1995	5	0	0	0	0	0
Willemse, AK (Ashwin)	Lions	2003, 2007	5	1	0	0	0	5
Williams, CM (Chester)	Western Province	1995	3	4	0	0	0	20

— WATSON THE RUGBY WORLD CUP FINAL REF —

André Watson, currently the Manager of Referees at SA Rugby, is the only referee that has officiated at more than one final in Rugby World Cup history. He was the man in the middle of the 1999 and 2003 finals. Here is a list of referees in RWC finals:

1987	Kerry Fitzgerald (Australia)	New Zealand beat France 29–9
1991	Derek Bevan (Wales)	Australia beat England 12–6
1995	Ed Morrison (England)	South Africa beat New Zealand 15–12
1999	André Watson (South Africa)	Australia beat France 35–12
2003	André Watson (South Africa)	England beat Australia 20–17
2007	Alain Rolland (Ireland)	South Africa beat England 15–6

— RUGBY UNION SCORING —

In 1886 scoring by points was introduced into the laws of the Rugby Football Union for the first time. Prior to this date, matches were decided by a majority of goals.

The table below shows the various points values during the applicable seasons from 1891, the year in which South Africa first participated in international rugby.

Era	Try	Conversion	Dropped Goal	Penalty Goal	Goal from a Mark*
1891	1	2	3	2	3
1892–93	2	3	4	3	4
1894–1905	3	2	4	3	4
1906–48	3	2	4	3	3
1949–71	3	2	3	3	3
1972–77	4	2	3	3	3
1978–92	4	2	3	3	–
1992–present	5	2	3	3	–

A goal from a mark was no longer possible when the free kick clause was introduced in 1978.

— SPRINGBOK RUGBY FIRSTS —

The first Springbok rugby international took place on Thursday, 30 July 1891 against Great Britain on the Port Elizabeth Cricket Club Ground, Port Elizabeth. South Africa conceded two tries and lost by 4–0. This was nearly twenty years after the very first international rugby match took place at the Academy Ground, Raeburn Place, Edinburgh on Monday, 27 March 1871 between England and Scotland.

The first Springbok captain was Herbert Hayton ('HH') Castens from Western Province. The referee on this historic occasion was Dr John Griffin, who was born in England and played once for Wales in 1883 against Scotland before he emigrated to South Africa.

The first Springbok victory came in their seventh international, namely the fourth test at Newlands, Cape Town against Great Britain on 5 September 1896. South Africa won by 5–0. South Africa wore green jerseys for the first time in this test. Prior to this they wore either club jerseys, the provincial jerseys of the city in which they were playing, or just plain jerseys.

The first Springbok try- and points-scorer was TA (Theo) Samuels of Griqualand West in the second test against Great Britain in 1896 at the Old Wanderers in Johannesburg. Samuels was a last-minute inclusion when wing Frank Maxwell of Transvaal had to withdraw because of injury. He also scored a second try later in the test. Such is fate; Maxwell is forgotten today, while Samuels will always have a special place in South African sports history.

The first South African to score with the boot was DG (Davie) Cope, the Transvaal fullback, when he converted Samuels's second try against Great Britain in 1896 in Johannesburg.

The first drawn match involving South Africa was at the Old Wanderers, Johannesburg, on Wednesday, 26 August 1903, when Great Britain and South Africa drew 10–10.

Charles (Hasie) and Marthinus (Oupa) Versfeld were the first set of brothers to play for the Springboks. 'Oupa' Versfeld played in all three internationals against the British Isles in 1891 and was joined by his brother Hasie in the third test on 5 September 1891 played at Newlands, Cape Town. Hasie Versfeld holds the distinction of scoring the only try against the British Isles on their first tour in 1891, in the opening match of the tour for the Cape Clubs against the visitors. Incidentally, four Versfeld brothers played against Great Britain on their tour in 1891, the above-mentioned two as well as John and Loftus, whose name has been given to the field at the headquarters of the Northern Transvaal Rugby Union (now Blue Bulls Rugby Union) in recognition of the sterling services he rendered to rugby in Pretoria.

The first South African selectors known to us selected the South African team for the final test in 1903. They were Barry Heatlie, Percy Jones and Biddy Anderson, all from Western Province, Villagers and Diocesan College.

Percy Allport, the Western Province wing and fullback, became the first South African fullback to score a try in a test when he scored against the British Isles in the third test at Newlands, Cape Town in 1910. Quite a few Springboks have played both wing and fullback for South Africa. They are: Theo Samuels, Arthur Marsberg, Gerry Brand, Freddy Turner, Jimmy White, Roy Dryburgh, Gavin Johnson, James Small, Percy Montgomery, Justin Swart, Breyton Paulse, Thinus Delport, Brent Russell, Jaque Fourie, Conrad Jantjes, JP Pietersen, Francois Steyn and Gio Aplon.

The first Springbok head – awarded to the first side to defeat a touring Springbok side – was handed to the Welsh club Newport when they beat the Springboks 9–3 on 24 October 1912.

The first Springbok to score a try against New Zealand was Attie van Heerden in the first test on 13 August 1921 in Dunedin. He also represented South Africa as a sprinter in the 1920 Olympic Games in Antwerp, Belgium.

The first dropped goal for South Africa was by Gerhard Morkel against New Zealand in the second test at Auckland on 27 August 1921. In those days the dropped kick was worth four points.

The first and only Springbok to kick a goal from a mark was Phil Mostert in the second test against New Zealand at Ellis Park in Johannesburg on 21 July 1928.

In the third test against New Zealand in 1928 in Port Elizabeth, the Springboks wore white shorts for the first time, the only reason being that this made it easier for the referee, VH (Boet) Neser, to identify the players. In 1937 the Springboks started playing with white shorts again; against the touring British Lions in 1938 the Springboks briefly reverted to black shorts, but permanently settled for white in 1949.

In 1933, for the first and only time in test history, the Springboks hosted a five-test series against the Wallabies, winning by three tests to two.

In 1949, for the first time in history, South Africa won all their tests at home – four games against the touring All Blacks.

Rhodesia produced its first Springboks in 1949 when Ryk van Schoor and Salty du Rand were both chosen for South Africa in the second test at Johannesburg. The 1912 Springbok Joe Francis from Transvaal was born in Gatooma in Rhodesia.

The Springboks first played against the Barbarians on the 1951–52 tour to the United Kingdom and France, winning 17–3 at Cardiff.

When Harry Walker (1953–56), the son of Alf Walker (1921–24), was selected for South Africa, they become the first father and son to play for South Africa.

The 1953 Wallabies were the first tourists to travel by air to and from South Africa.

In 1955, Sias Swart, a wing, became the first player from South West Africa to play for the Springboks – against the touring British Lions team.

When the 1956 Springboks went to Australia and New Zealand, they became the first Springbok team to fly to the country in which they toured.

In 1958 the French touring side visited South Africa on the first major tour ever undertaken by a French team. The French side designed a blazer and tie to mark the occasion, something they had never done before. This

was the first time a visiting team completed all its travel by air, apart from visiting the Kruger National Park by rail. It was also the first time since 1896 that South Africa lost a test series against a touring team.

The first penalty try awarded to South Africa in a test was in the second test against Australia at Newlands in Cape Town on 10 August 1963, when Tommy Bedford was obstructed by Beres Ellwood early in the match during a chase following a kick by Jannie Engelbrecht. The referee was a South African, Mr PA (Toy) Myburgh.

Norman Sanson from Scotland became the first neutral referee in a test match in South Africa when he took charge of both internationals against France in 1975.

Thys Burger became the first Springbok substitute to score a try in a test after replacing Theuns Stofberg in the game against the United States in Glenville, New York on 25 September 1981.

The Springboks conceded their first penalty try ever in a test against the New Zealand Cavaliers in the first test at Newlands on 10 May 1986. The referee was Mr Ken Rowlands of Wales.

South Africa became World Champions for the first time on 24 June 1995 when they won the Webb Ellis Trophy with a 15–12 victory over New Zealand in the final at Ellis Park, Johannesburg.

— OUR FIRST SPRINGBOK CAPTAIN —

This honour belongs to Herbert Hayton ('HH') Castens from Western Province. He led South Africa in the first international against the British Isles on 30 July 1891 in Port Elizabeth, in the days when the team was usually selected by the home Union. It may at first therefore seem strange that Castens, who was from Western Province, was chosen. However, the President of the Eastern Province Rugby Union at that stage was Emile Castens, his father!

'HH' was born in Pearston in the Eastern Cape and educated at Rugby School, England before proceeding to Oxford University where he studied law and where he also obtained his rugby 'blue' in 1886 and 1887. Returning to South Africa, he practised as a lawyer and later became secretary to the Rhodesian (now Zimbabwean) Government. He married Mary Jane Little, whose brother Edward Little was another who appeared in the first test match played in South Africa. In 1894 'HH' also captained the first Springbok cricket team to tour Britain and Ireland. They were the first South African team to appear at Lord's cricket ground where they played against – and beat – a team captained by none other than the famous WG Grace.

'HH' was the referee in the third test against the British Isles in 1891, played at Newlands in Cape Town. His brother, GE (Emile) Castens, also played against the touring side when he represented Port Elizabeth and Eastern Province. Oddly enough the referee in both matches was 'HH' Castens.

— IN OPPOSITION —

South Africa has faced 24 different opponents over the years, with five of those not actually being single countries: British and Irish Lions (and their forerunners), World Invitation XV, South America & Spain, New Zealand Cavaliers and Pacific Islanders.

Opponent	First Meeting	Tests	W	L	D
Lions*	30 Jul 1891 (Port Elizabeth)	46	23	17	6
Scotland	17 Nov 1906 (Glasgow)	21	16	5	–
Ireland	24 Nov 1906 (Belfast)	20	15	4	1
Wales	1 Dec 1906 (Swansea)	25	23	1	1
England	8 Dec 1906 (Crystal Palace)	32	19	12	1
France	11 Jan 1913 (Bordeaux)	38	21	11	6
New Zealand	13 Aug 1921 (Dunedin)	81	33	45	3
Australia	8 Jul 1933 (Cape Town)	71	41	29	1
World Invitation XV	27 Aug 1977 (Pretoria)	3	3	–	–
South America**	26 Apr 1980 (Johannesburg)	8	7	1	–
United States	25 Sep 1981 (Glenville)	3	3	–	–
NZ Cavaliers	10 May 1986 (Durban)	4	3	1	–
Argentina	6 Nov 1993 (Buenos Aires)	13	13	–	–
Western Samoa#	13 Apr 1995 (Johannesburg)	6	6	–	–
Romania	30 May 1995 (Cape Town)	1	1	–	–
Canada	3 Jun 1995 (Port Elizabeth)	2	2	–	–
Italy	12 Nov 1995 (Rome)	10	10	–	
Fiji	2 Jul 1996 (Pretoria)	2	2	–	–
Tonga	10 Jun 1997 (Cape Town)	2	2	–	–

Opponent	First Meeting	Tests	W	L	D
Spain	10 Oct 1999 (Edinburgh)	1	1	–	–
Uruguay	15 Oct 1999 (Glasgow)	3	3	–	–
Georgia	24 Oct 2003 (Sydney)	1	1	–	–
Pacific Islanders	17 Jul 2004 (Gosford)	1	1	–	–
Namibia	15 Aug 2007 (Cape Town)	1	1	–	–

Western Samoa became simply Samoa in 1998.

* Including games against Great Britain and the British and Irish Lions.

** South America in 1984 also featured guest players from Spain!

— SPRINGBOK LEGENDS: BENNIE OSLER —

Benjamin Louwrens (Bennie) Osler was born on 23 November 1901 at Aliwal North, where his father was a practising attorney. He matriculated at Kingswood College in Grahamstown. After school he attended the University of Cape Town where he quickly graduated from under-19 level to the senior team as a flyhalf. He played his first game for Western Province at the age of 20 in 1922. In 1924 he played in all four tests against the British touring team and played his last test against the touring Wallabies in the fifth test of the 1933 series. In the first test against New Zealand in 1928 his brother Stanley made his first and only appearance in a test match. In 1931 Bennie was chosen as captain of the Springbok side to Great Britain. In 1933 he was dropped as captain against the Wallabies in favour of Philip Nel, but captained the side in the second test in the absence of the injured Nel.

The talented flyhalf and kicking genius dominated South African rugby during the middle and late twenties and into the early thirties. Besides his tactical kicking on attack and in defence, Bennie was also a great placekicker and a dropped goal artist. With great speed off the mark, Bennie could also break when the occasion presented itself. In Bennie's days the dropped goal counted four points, and thanks to his quick thinking and twinkling feet he would drop a quick goal rather than pass to doubtful or off-form centres. Bennie regarded the game as one of possession and speed, and if that ball did not come quickly enough from a scrum or line-out, Bennie would kick for touch no matter the feelings of spectators.

Dr Danie Craven had this to say about his halfback partner from 1931 to 1933: 'He was a difficult man to play with, but that is the way it is when you come across a genius like Bennie; you had to follow blindly, believing and trusting that he would do the right thing. This Bennie Osler seldom failed to do on the rugby field.'

BENNIE OSLER FACTFILE
Born: 23 November 1901 at Aliwal North, Eastern Cape
Province: Western Province
Caps: 17 (W12, D1, L4)
Scoring: 46 points (2 tries, 6 conversions, 4 penalties, 4 dropped goals)
Springbok debut: vs Great Britain on 16 August 1924 in Durban

Bennie Osler putting the Springboks on the attack.

— SUCCESSFUL SCHOOLS —

When Heinrich Brüssow was chosen for the Springboks on their tour to Wales, Scotland and England at the end of the 2008 season, he became the 38th player from the rugby 'factory' in Bloemfontein that is Grey College, which has produced the most Springboks. Diocesan College in Cape Town, with 34 Springboks, is in second place. Most of Bishops' (as Diocesan College is also known) Springboks were selected before the Second World War.

Here's a list of the schools and colleges that have produced the most Springbok test players:

School/College	Players
Grey College, Bloemfontein	38
Diocesan College, Cape Town (Bishops)	35
Paul Roos Gymnasium, Stellenbosch	32
South African College Schools (SACS)	20
Paarl Gymnasium	19
Kimberley Boys High	16
Paarl Boys High	16
Rondebosch Boys High	14
Maritzburg College	10

In 1977 four ex-pupils of Grey College in Bloemfontein, namely Morné du Plessis (captain), Theuns Stofberg, Dawie Snyman and Robbie Blair, played together for the Springboks against the World XV. In 2004 this feat was equalled when four ex-pupils of Paarl Gymnasium played together for the Springboks: they were Marius Joubert, De Wet Barry, Jean de Villiers and Schalk Burger.

— BREWIS THE LUCKY CHARM —

Johannes Daniel 'Hannes' Brewis, the Northern Transvaal flyhalf, holds a remarkable Springbok record of having played in ten successive tests between 1949 and 1953, all of which were victories. His test career began with the visit of the All Blacks in 1949 in which they were despatched for the only time in their history 4–0. There followed wins over Scotland, Ireland, Wales, England and France on the grand slam tour of 1951–52, before rounding off his career with a 25–3 victory over Australia at Johannesburg in August 1953. He also appeared in the Springbok jersey in nine other touring matches, only one of which, against London Counties at Twickenham in 1951, ended in defeat.

— HIGHEST WINNING PERCENTAGE AS A SPRINGBOK —

Qualification: 20 or more tests

Name	Caps	Won	Lost	Drawn	% Wins
Adrian Garvey	28	24	4	–	86%
Morné du Plessis	22	18	4	–	82%
James Dalton	43	35	8	–	81%
Theuns Stofberg	21	17	4	–	81%
Gerrie Germishuys	20	16	4	–	80%
Louis Moolman	24	19	5	–	79%
Gurthrö Steenkamp	31	23	8	–	74%
Bismarck du Plessis	36	26	10	–	72%
Jaque Fourie	62	44	18	–	71%

— WINLESS ROUX —

Ockert Antonie 'Tonie' Roux, the Northern Transvaal centre/fullback, never tasted that winning feeling in seven Springbok test caps between 1969 and 1974, although incredibly three of those matches were drawn. His test career began with a defeat to Scotland at Murrayfield, a loss to England and draws with Ireland and Wales. He was then on the losing side against England at Ellis Park in 1972, and during the 1974 visit of the British Lions he was recalled for the 3rd and 4th tests, which ended in a defeat and a draw. Roux was an unused bench replacement a further 13 times in which South Africa had a record of 11 won, 1 drawn, and 1 lost.

— LOWEST WINNING PERCENTAGE AS A SPRINGBOK —

Qualification: 20 or more tests

Name	Caps	Won	Lost	Drawn	% Win
Braam van Straaten	21	9	11	1	43%
De Wet Barry	39	18	20	1	46%
Corné Krige	39	18	21	0	46%
Eddie Andrews	23	11	11	1	48%
Cobus Visagie	29	14	14	1	48%

— GROUND FORCE – 50 POINTS AT ONE STADIUM —

Percy Montgomery, who scored by far the most points for South Africa in its test history, holds the record of scoring the most test points at Newlands in Cape Town, Loftus Versfeld in Pretoria, Ellis Park in Johannesburg, the Absa Stadium in Durban and the EP Rugby Football Union Ground in Port Elizabeth. He scored the most test points at one stadium at Newlands in Cape Town, for many years his home ground. Naas Botha scored 56 points at his home ground, Loftus Versfeld, in just four outings.

The following is a list of most points per venue:

Pts	Stadium	Name	Starts+Reps
108	Newlands, Cape Town	Percy Montgomery	9
105	Loftus Versfeld, Pretoria	Percy Montgomery	9+1
86	Ellis Park, Johannesburg	Percy Montgomery	6+3
73	Absa Stadium, Durban	Percy Montgomery	7+2
61	EPRFU Ground, Port Elizabeth	Percy Montgomery	4
59	Murrayfield, Edinburgh	Percy Montgomery	5
56	Loftus Versfeld, Pretoria	Naas Botha	4
54	Stade de France, Paris	Percy Montgomery	5+1
53	Ellis Park, Johannesburg	Joel Stransky	4+1

— CHESTER'S EIGHT IN JOHANNESBURG —

Ellis Park in Johannesburg was Chester Williams' happiest hunting ground. The speedy wing scored eight of his 14 test tries at this venue, including four tries against Western Samoa in 1995 in the quarter-final of the Rugby World Cup.

The following is a list of five and more tries at one venue in a career:

Tries	Stadium	Name	Starts+Reps
8	Ellis Park, Johannesburg	Chester Williams	5
7	Absa Stadium, Durban	Stefan Terblanche	3
6	Absa Stadium, East London	Tonderai Chavhanga	1
5	EPRFU Ground, Port Elizabeth	Breyton Paulse	3
5	Loftus Versfeld, Pretoria	Pieter Rossouw	4+1
5	Loftus Versfeld, Pretoria	Percy Montgomery	9+1
5	Loftus Versfeld, Pretoria	Danie Gerber	4
5	Ellis Park, Johannesburg	Hennie van Zyl	2
5	Ellis Park, Johannesburg	Breyton Paulse	5+1
5	Ellis Park, Johannesburg	Jongi Nokwe	2
5	Ellis Park, Johannesburg	Danie Gerber	3
5	Ferrocarril Oeste, Buenos Aires	James Small	4

— JOOST, TOP MAN AT ELLIS PARK, AND VICTOR AT NEWLANDS —

Joost van der Westhuizen, who held the South African record for most test matches with 89 before Percy Montgomery surpassed it in 2007, and Victor Matfield, who holds the current South African record with 105 caps, are the two players who have appeared in the most test matches at one venue, 11 at Ellis Park and 11 at Newlands. Van der Westhuizen also played in 10 test matches on his home ground Loftus Versfeld in Pretoria, the same number as Percy Montgomery.

The following is a list of most caps per stadium:

Caps	Stadium	Name	Starts+Reps
11	Ellis Park, Johannesburg	Joost van der Westhuizen	11
11	Newlands, Cape Town	Victor Matfield	11
10	Loftus Versfeld, Pretoria	Joost van der Westhuizen	10
10	Loftus Versfeld, Pretoria	Percy Montgomery	9+1
10	Ellis Park, Johannesburg	Mark Andrews	10
9	Ellis Park, Johannesburg	Percy Montgomery	6+3
9	Ellis Park, Johannesburg	Os du Randt	9
9	Absa Stadium, Durban	Percy Montgomery	7+2
9	Newlands, Cape Town	Joost van der Westhuizen	8+1
9	Newlands, Cape Town	Percy Montgomery	9
9	Newlands, Cape Town	Os du Randt	9
9	Newlands, Cape Town	Victor Matfield	9

— THE POPULARITY OF CAPE TOWN —

Cape Town is a very popular place for Springboks to be born in: no less than 46 test-playing Springboks have been born in this city. Second on this list is Johannesburg and Pretoria with 32 players each.

Birthplace	Players
Cape Town	46
Johannesburg	32
Pretoria	32

Birthplace	Players
Kimberley	25
Paarl	22
Bloemfontein	19
Port Elizabeth	16
Durban	15
Stellenbosch	14

Although many Springboks have been born in metropolitan areas (Cape Town, Port Elizabeth, Durban, Gauteng and Bloemfontein), the rural districts also produced their fair share of Springboks.

Some of the more prolific smaller towns which have produced Springboks include:

Birthplace	Players
Ceres	9
George	7
Potchefstroom	7
Somerset East	7
Bethlehem	6
Harrismith	6
Kroonstad	6
Steynsburg	6
Aliwal North	5
Caledon	5
Calvinia	5
Cradock	5
Moorreesburg	5
Nelspruit	5
Oudtshoorn	5
Senekal	5
Victoria West	5
Welkom	5
Worcester	5

— PIONEER DAY —

Rugby football was played in South Africa from at least as early as the 1860s. The game was firmly established by 1889 when the South African Rugby Board was constituted as the governing body. TB Herold, then honorary secretary of the Western Province Rugby Union, was the first to suggest that a touring team from Britain be invited to tour the country, and with the support of Bill Simkins, his president, contact was made with the Rugby Football Union in England. The project was approved after lengthy negotiations. Cecil John Rhodes, then Prime Minister of the Cape Colony, offered to cover any possible financial loss, and in April 1891 it was duly announced that Scotsman WE (Bill) McLagan would visit South Africa with a team of 20 other players drawn from the unions of England and Scotland.

The first Springbok international rugby match was held on Thursday, 30 July 1891 against the British Isles on the Cricket Club Ground in St George's Park, Port Elizabeth, where 'the pavilion was again crowded with ladies, all intent on the game' (*Cape Times*). Much was expected from the South African team, and the crowd of 6 000 were not disappointed in the football produced that day. South Africa conceded two tries and lost 4–0. It was an overcast day in Port Elizabeth and the ground was level with grass on it, one of the only fields in South Africa where the team from Britain played on grass.

The first Springbok captain was Herbert Hayton ('HH') Castens from Western Province. He led the following team: Ben Duff, Mosey van Buuren, 'Chubb' Vigne, Harry Boyes, Alf Richards, Frank Guthrie, 'Oupa' Versfeld, William Bissett, 'HH' Castens (Captain), Tiger Devenish, Japie Louw, Edward Little, Fred Alexander, George Merry and George Hamilton. The team consisted of nine forwards and six backs. The referee on this historic occasion was Dr John Griffin, an English-born gentleman who played for Wales once in 1883 against Scotland before he emigrated to South Africa. South Africa wore the white Crusader club jersey. Castens was often prominent with 'grand rushes' in a game contested mainly by the forwards. Ben Duff and 'Chubb' Vigne also played well for South Africa, and Alf Richards was described as the best halfback on the field. Generally the British backs were far more sophisticated, however, and Aston and Whittaker 'planted tries', with Rotherham converting one to make the final score 4–0.

— DAN THE MAN —

Daniel Carter, the New Zealand flyhalf, leads the way as the most successful Springbok slayer of them all, with an average of 15 points per game in his 15 matches against South Africa.

Here's a list of all those who have scored over a century of points against South Africa in tests.

Name	Country	M	T	C	PG	DG	Pts
Daniel Carter	New Zealand	14+1	3	25	61	1	221
Andrew Mehrtens	New Zealand	14+2	–	19	53	4	209
Stirling Mortlock	Australia	16+1	7	17	27	–	150
Matt Burke	Australia	12+4	1	12	36	1	140
Jonny Wilkinson	England	8+1	–	5	36	3	127
Neil Jenkins	Wales	9+2	–	4	35	–	113

— TWO COUNTRIES AGAINST THE BOKS —

Many players have appeared for two different teams against South Africa, but if you exclude amalgamated sides like the British and Irish Lions, Pacific Islanders and South America, then just two players have appeared for two separate countries against the Boks:

Patricio Noriega played four games at prop for Argentina (1993–94) and five for Australia (1999–2003) against South Africa.

Shane Howarth competed in three tests at fullback for New Zealand (1994) and then two more for Wales (1998–99).

— FOR AND AGAINST —

Only two players have appeared for and against South Africa in tests.

Toronto-born Christian Stewart played at the centre for Canada against the Springboks during the 1995 World Cup clash at Port Elizabeth, and gained 14 caps for the country of his birth. He then swapped allegiance to the country where he grew up and went to school, winning three further caps for South Africa against Scotland, Ireland and England on the 1998 tour.

Tiaan Strauss won the first of his 15 Springbok caps against France in Lyon in 1992, and was captain in two of those games. Then, after the 1995 Currie Cup final, he signed to play rugby league in Australia for the Cronulla Sharks.

Tiaan made just 14 appearances in the 13-man code over the next two seasons. Staying in Sydney, he returned to Union and played for the Waratahs in the Super 12. Residency rules allowed him to make his Wallaby debut against Ireland in 1999. He made two replacement appearances for Australia against South Africa during the 1999 Tri-Nations in Brisbane and Cape Town and went on to make 11 test appearances for Australia.

— GRAND SLAM TOURS —

South Africa have embarked on nine tours in which they have played each of the Five Nations of England, France, Ireland, Scotland and Wales. On two occasions – in 1912–13 and 1951–52 – they returned home having achieved a Grand Slam of victories. Only one other tour encompassed tests against all Five Nations: in 1960–61 the Springboks beat Wales, Ireland, England and Scotland before drawing 0–0 with France.

— PROLIFIC PERCY —

With his 140 points against Australia in 20 tests, Percy Montgomery holds the South African record of scoring the most test points against one country in a career. He also scored the most points in tests against New Zealand, Scotland, England, Wales, France and Ireland. Naas Botha scored an amazing 69 points against the New Zealand Cavaliers in 4 tests, with an average of 17,25 per match.

The following is a list of most points per player against opponents:

Points	Opponent	Name	Starts+Reps
140	Australia	Percy Montgomery	17+3
106	New Zealand	Percy Montgomery	18+1
101	Scotland	Percy Montgomery	7
99	England	Percy Montgomery	12
91	Wales	Percy Montgomery	7+2
78	France	Percy Montgomery	7+2

Points	Opponent	Name	Starts+Reps
69	NZ Cavaliers	Naas Botha	4
65	South America	Naas Botha	6
64	Australia	Piet Visagie	7
64	Australia	Joel Stransky	5
62	Australia	Jannie de Beer	4
56	Ireland	Percy Montgomery	6
56	England	Braam van Straaten	4
54	New Zealand	Joel Stransky	5+1
54	Australia	Braam van Straaten	5
53	France	Henry Honiball	4

— DANIE LIKES SOUTH AMERICA —

Danie Gerber must have liked playing against the South Americans: he scored eight tries against them in only six tests! This includes a hat-trick in 1982 at Loftus Versfeld in Pretoria. Breyton Paulse liked scoring against the Australians, with seven tries against them, and Chester Williams scored six tries against the hapless Samoans in only two tests, scoring four in the quarter-final of the 1995 Rugby World Cup.

The following is a list of most tries per player against opponents:

Tries	Opponent	Name	Starts+Reps
8	South America	Danie Gerber	6
7	Australia	Breyton Paulse	14+3
6	Samoa	Chester Williams	2
6	Wales	Joost van der Westhuizen	6
6	Uruguay	Tonderai Chavhanga	1
6	South America	Ray Mordt	8
6	New Zealand	Joost van der Westhuizen	15+2
6	Italy	Stefan Terblanche	1+1
6	France	Pieter Rossouw	3
6	England	Bryan Habana	7+1

— FIFTEEN GAMES AGAINST ONE OPPONENT —

Victor Matfield played 23 test matches against New Zealand in his career. This is the most by a South African player against any opponent. The following is a list of most test matches against opponents by a Springbok player:

Caps	Opponent	Name	Starts+Reps
23	New Zealand	Victor Matfield	22+1
22	Australia	Victor Matfield	22
20	Australia	Percy Montgomery	17+3
19	New Zealand	Percy Montgomery	18+1
19	New Zealand	Mark Andrews	18+1
18	New Zealand	Os du Randt	18
17	New Zealand	Joost van der Westhuizen	15+2
17	Australia	Breyton Paulse	14+3
15	Australia	Joost van der Westhuizen	11+4
15	Australia	Os du Randt	15
15	Australia	John Smit	10+5
12	England	Percy Montgomery	12
10	France	Jan Ellis	10
9	Wales	Percy Montgomery	7+2
9	Wales	Victor Matfield	8+1

— TAKE A BREAK —

In 1974 the Springbok selectors chose Roy McCallum at scrumhalf for the third test against the British Lions in Port Elizabeth on 13 July. He withdrew due to injury and because Paul Bayvel was also injured, the selectors opted to fly three scrumhalves – Barry Wolmarans, Gert Schutte and Gerrie Sonnekus – to Port Elizabeth to practise with the team before making their final decision. They chose Gerrie Sonnekus to play with his halfback partner from Free State, Jackie Snyman. Sonnekus played at eightman for the University of the Orange Free State in 1973 but decided to switch to scrumhalf in the beginning of 1974. He made his debut (at scrumhalf) for Free State on 27 April 1974 against Rhodesia and he also played scrumhalf for Free State against the British Lions on 29 June. It is a misconception that he was played out of position. In 1975 Sonnekus switched back to eightman again. Ten years after making his Springboks debut, Sonnekus once again played for the Springboks on 2 June 1984 against England, this time at eightman.

— MOST TESTS MISSED —

The record for the most Springbok test matches missed between appearances is held by Adi Jacobs. His remarkable sojourn lasted almost six years between gaining his 10th cap on 23 November 2002 against England at Twickenham until his 11th on 7 June 2008 versus Wales in Bloemfontein. In the intervening period the Springboks played 66 official test matches.

No	Name	From	To
66	Adrian Jacobs	10th cap (23 Nov 2002)	11th cap (8 Jun 2008)
63	Johan Ackermann	8th cap (28 Jul 2001)	9th cap (11 Nov 2006)
60	Johan Ackermann	4th cap (3 Aug 1996)	5th cap (23 Jun 2001)
57	Toks van der Linde	6th cap (15 Dec 1996)	7th cap (10 Nov 2001)
53	Gaffie du Toit	6th cap (7 Aug 1999)	7th cap (12 Jun 2004)
50	Wayne Julies	debut (10 Oct 1999)	2nd cap (12 Jun 2004)

— MOST TIME BETWEEN TEST APPEARANCES —

Time	Name	From	To	Tests missed
9y 325d	Gerrie Sonnekus	debut (13 Jul 1974)	2nd cap (2 Jun 1984)	28
9y 242d	Rudi Visagie	4th cap (27 Oct 1984)	5th cap (26 Jun 1993)	12
8y 214d	Boy Morkel	6th cap (11 Jan 1913)	7th cap (13 Aug 1921)	1

8y 214d	Gerhard Morkel	5th cap (11 Jan 1913)	6th cap (13 Aug 1921)	1
7y 145d	Burger Geldenhuys	5th cap (3 Apr 1982)	6th cap (26 Aug 1989)	9
6y 362d	Jackie Powell	2nd cap (29 Aug 1896)	3rd cap (26 Aug 1903)	2

— SPRINGBOKS IN OTHER SPORTS —

HH Castens (1 cap, 1891): Captain of the 1895 SA cricket touring side to England; the 24 games on tour were not first-class and did not include tests.

AR (Alf) Richards (3 caps, 1891): Captain of SA cricket team in the 3rd test against England at Cape Town in March 1896, scoring 6 and 0.

AW (Bertie) Powell (1 cap, 1896): Played cricket for SA in the 2nd test against England at Newlands in April 1899, scoring 5 and 11 and taking one wicket.

PST (Percy) Jones (3 caps, 1896): Played cricket for SA in the 3rd test against Australia at Cape Town in November 1902, bagging a pair on his only appearance.

JH (Biddy) Anderson (3 caps, 1896): Skippered SA in the 2nd cricket test against Australia at the Old Wanderers, Johannesburg in October 1902, scoring 32 and 11.

JH (Jimmy) Sinclair (1 cap, 1903): Played in 25 cricket tests for SA between 1896 and 1911, tallying 1 069 runs at an average of 23,23 including 3 centuries, and taking 63 wickets at an average of 31,68 with a best in an innings of 9 for 89.

J (Attie) van Heerden (2 caps, 1921): Represented SA in the 400-metre hurdles at the 1920 Olympic Games in Antwerp, Belgium.

TA (Tony) Harris (5 caps, 1937-38): Played cricket for SA in three tests between 1947 and 1949, scoring 100 runs in 5 innings.

J (Poens) Prinsloo (1 cap, 1963): Also a Springbok in athletics.

J (Jaco) Reinach (4 caps, 1986): Also a Springbok in athletics, he broke the SA 400-metre record in 1983 with a time of 45,01 seconds. This record stood for 15 years.

Daan Ackermann (0 caps, 1970): Benched for SA in the second test against NZ in 1970. Also a Springbok in amateur wrestling.

— SPRINGBOK SPORTING WIVES —

Springboks whose wives also became Springboks:
Felix du Plessis and **Pat** (*née* Smethurst) – hockey
Des Sinclair and **Jill** (*née* Abraham) – hockey
John Wessels and **Sussie** (*née* Esterhuizen) – netball
Dick Lockyear and **Rhona** (*née* Kirkpatrick) – hockey
Ian Kirkpatrick and **Norma** (*née* Doubell/Little) – hockey
Lofty Nel and **Hester** (*née* Muller) – jukskei
Gert Muller and **Letitia** (*née* Malan) – athletics
Joggie Jansen and **Rista** (*née* Joubert) – equestrian endurance races
Naas Botha and **Karen** (*née* Kruger) – athletics (competed in long jump at the 1992 Barcelona Olympics)
Pierre Edwards and **Aryna** (*née* Lombard) – hockey
Niel Hugo and **Rese** (*née* Malan) – netball
Os du Randt and **Hannelie** (*née* Vermeulen) – swimming

— HARRIS'S ELLIS PARK DOUBLE —

Tony Harris, the Transvaal flyhalf, is the only person to have played test rugby and test cricket at Ellis Park in Johannesburg, having scored a try against the British Lions there during a 26–12 victory in July 1938, and then scoring 6 (bowled by Alec Bedser) and 1 not out against England at the ground over a decade later in February 1949.

Jimmy Sinclair did the same at the Old Wanderers in Johannesburg, appearing in eight cricket tests at the venue between 1896 and 1910, with his only rugby cap being sandwiched in between on 26 August 1903 as a forward against the British Isles. This game came just ten months after he scored a century there against Australia. Sinclair also took 8 for 70 at the ground with his medium pacers in the 2nd innings and 12 wickets in the game against England in March 1906.

The only other player from any country to have ever played test cricket and test rugby on the same pitch is 'Monkey' Hornby (for England at the Oval in London), although Brian McKechnie (for New Zealand at the Sydney Cricket Ground, Lancaster Park in Christchurch and Eden Park in Auckland) and Jeff Wilson (for New Zealand at Carisbrook in Dunedin and Eden Park in Auckland) have played test rugby and one-day international cricket on the exact same piece of turf.

— SPRINGBOK LEGENDS: DANIE CRAVEN —

Daniël Hartman (Danie) Craven is often called Mr Rugby in South Africa and rightly so. He played a big part in South African rugby as a player, captain, selector, coach and finally as the President of the South African Rugby Board for nearly 38 years. He grew up in Lindley in the Eastern Free State, where he matriculated in 1928. After matric he went to Stellenbosch University as a theological student. In 1931 he was chosen for the Springboks tour to the United Kingdom, before he even played for Western Province. On this tour he played in three of the four tests, at the expense of Pierre de Villiers, who incidentally was also from Western Province. In his test career of 16 tests, which was cut short by the Second World War, Craven represented South Africa in four positions: scrumhalf, flyhalf, centre and eightman, one of only two players in the history of SA Rugby to gain selection as a forward and a back. He also played fullback in a midweek game in New Zealand in 1937. In 1938 he was chosen as captain of the Springboks against the touring Great Britain team, a series won by South Africa. When the Springboks returned to the international scene in 1949, Danie Craven was chosen as one of the selectors and also coached the team. On the 1951–52 tour to the United Kingdom and France he was the assistant manager and, as was customary in those days, also the coach. In 1956 he became the President of the SA Rugby Board, a position he held until his death on 4 January 1993.

DANIE CRAVEN FACTFILE
Born: 11 October 1910, Lindley, Orange Free State
Provinces: Western Province, Eastern Province, Northern Transvaal
Caps: 16 (W12, D0, L4)
Scoring: 6 points (2 tries)
Springbok debut: vs Wales on 5 December 1931 at Swansea

Danie Craven did not invent the dive-pass, but he perfected it.

— GREATEST COMEBACKS —

South Africa have overturned a deficit of more than ten points to win a game in only seven test matches, the best of which was when they trailed by 18 points with just 13 minutes left against the All Blacks in Durban in 1998 and won 24–23.

Margin	Opponents (Venue)	Date	Details
18	New Zealand (Durban)	15 Aug 1998	SA trailing 5–23 after 67', won 24–23
14	Wales (Wembley)	14 Nov 1998	SA trailing 0–14 after 32', won 28–20
13	Scotland (Durban)	7 Jun 2003	SA trailing 12–25 after 62', won 29–25
11	New Zealand (Christchurch)	4 Sep 1965	SA trailing 5–16 after 45', won 19–16
11	England (Twickenham)	29 Nov 1997	SA trailing 0–11 after 40', won 29–11
11	England (Twickenham)	25 Nov 2006	SA trailing 3–14 after 33', won 25–14
11	British and Irish Lions (Pretoria)	27 June 2009	SA trailing 5–16 after 40', won 28–25

— LARGEST CAPITULATIONS —

South Africa have relinquished a lead of more than ten points to lose a game in only six test matches, the worst of which was when they led by 17 points with over a quarter of the game gone against the Wallabies in Sydney in June 2007, but then conceded 25 unanswered points and lost 17–25.

Margin	Opponents (Venue)	Date	Details
17	Australia (Sydney)	7 Jul 2007	SA leading 17–0 after 23', lost 17–25
16	New Zealand (Johannesburg)	19 Jul 1997	SA leading 23–7 after 36', lost 32–35

Margin	Opponents (Venue)	Date	Details
12	New Zealand (Cape Town)	10 Aug 1996	SA leading 18–6 after 60', lost 18–29
12	France (Cape Town)	24 Jun 2006	SA leading 23–11 after 53', lost 26–36
12	England (Twickenham)	18 Nov 2006	SA leading 18–6 after 49', lost 21–23
11	Australia (Cape Town)	5 Sep 1953	SA leading 14–3, after 45', lost 14–18
10	New Zealand (Auckland)	9 Aug 1997	SA leading 21–11 after 33', lost 35–55
10	Great Britain (Cape Town)	10 Sep 1938	SA leading 13–3 after 42', lost 16–21

— FIFTY UNANSWERED POINTS —

The Springboks tallied 170 points in a period during which the opposition failed to score, between the penalty goal by Italy's Francesco Mazzariol in the 10th minute of their 3–74 loss to South Africa at Port Elizabeth in June 1999, through the next game, which was a 101–0 victory for the Boks over Italy, until Neil Jenkins scored a penalty goal for Wales in the 1st minute of the test in Cardiff later that month.

The only time that South Africa have conceded more than 50 unanswered points began just after Percy Montgomery scored a penalty goal in the 68th minute of the Newlands test against France in June 2006, through the whole of the next game, which was the record 0–49 defeat to Australia in Brisbane, until Fourie du Preez scored a try after just 15 seconds against New Zealand in Wellington the next week.

For South Africa:

Pts	Opponents	Timescale
170	Italy	12 Jun 1999 (Port Elizabeth) to 19 Jun 1999 (Durban)
97	Uruguay	11 Jun 2005 (East London)
86	Samoa/England	9 Sep 2007 (Paris) to 14 Sep 2007 (Paris)
63	Argentina	9 Aug 2008 (Johannesburg)

60	GB/Scot/Ire/Wales	3 Sep 1910 (Cape Town) to 14 Dec 1912 (Cardiff)
55	Canada/Samoa	3 Jun 1995 (Port Elizabeth) to 10 Jun 1995 (Johannesburg)
53	Uruguay	11 Oct 2003 (Perth)

Against:

Pts	Opponents	Timescale
57	France/Australia	24 Jun 2006 (Cape Town) to 15 Jul 2006 (Brisbane)

— OH BROTHER —

Siblings who have played rugby for South Africa:

Three brothers

Luyt, FP (7 caps, 1910–13), **RR** (7 caps, 1910–13) and **JD** (4 caps, 1912–13)

The three Luyt brothers played together in three test matches on the 1912–13 tour, against Scotland, Wales and England.

Bekker, HPJ (15 caps, 1951–56), **RP** (2 caps, 1953) and **MJ** (1 cap, 1960)

Jaap and **Dolf Bekker** played together in the 3rd and 4th tests against Australia in 1953, both scoring a try in the 3rd test.

Du Plessis, W (14 caps, 1980–82), **CJ** (12 caps, 1981–89) and **MJ** (8 caps, 1984–89)

Willie and **Carel** played together in the two test against South America in 1982, both scoring a try in the 1st test.

Carel and Michael played together in eight test matches, both tests against South America and Spain in 1984, all four tests against the New Zealand Cavaliers in 1986 and both tests against a World XV in 1989.

Two brothers

Versfeld, M (3 caps, 1891) and **C** (1 cap, 1891)

Played together in the 3rd test against the British Isles in 1891.

Powell, JM (4 caps, 1891–1903) and **AW** (1 cap, 1896)

Played together in the 3rd test against the British Isles in 1896.

Devenish, GE (1 cap, 1891) and **CE** (1 cap, 1896)

Van Renen, CG (3 caps, 1891–96) and **WA** (2 caps, 1903)

Morkel, WS (4 caps, 1906) and **DFT** (9 caps, 1906–13)

Played together in the tests against Ireland and England in 1906.

Also played together in nine tour matches.

Reid, Alec (1903) and **Oupa** (1906)

Le Roux, JS (0 caps, 1906) and **PA** (3 caps, 1906)

Played together in six tour matches in 1906.

Marsberg, AFWD (3 caps, 1906) and **PA** (1 cap, 1910)

Roos, PJ (4 caps, 1903–06) and **GD** (2 caps, 1910)

Walker, Henry (3 caps, 1910) and **Alf** (6 caps, 1921–24)

Stegmann, AC (2 caps, 1906) and **JA** (5 caps, 1912–13)

Morkel, PG (8 caps, 1912–21) and **JWH** (5 caps, 1912–13)

Played together in all five tests on the 1912–13 tour to the British Isles and France.

Also played together in ten tour matches.

Krige, JD (5 caps, 1903–06) and **WA** (0 caps, 1912–13)

Morkel, JA (2 caps, 1921) and **HJL** (1 cap, 1921)

Played together in six tour matches on tour to Australia and New Zealand in 1921.

Walker, HW (3 caps, 1910) and **AP** (6 caps, 1921–24)

Osler, BL (17 caps, 1924–133) and **SG** (1 cap, 1928)

Played together in the 1st test against New Zealand in 1928.

Van der Westhuizen, JC (4 caps, 1928–32) and **JH** (3 caps, 1931–32)

Played together in the test against Ireland in 1932.

Also played together in six tour matches.

Louw, MM (18 caps, 1928–38) and **SC** (12 caps, 1931–38)

Played together in all five tests against Australia in 1933.

Played together in the 1st test against Australia and the 2nd and 3rd tests against New Zealand in 1937.

Played together in all three tests against the British Isles in 1938.

Also played together in ten tour matches to Australia and New Zealand in 1937.

Fry, DJ (0 caps, 1951–52) and **SP** (13 caps, 1951–55)

Played together in eight tour matches on the 1951–52 tour to the British Isles and France.

Wessels, PW (0 caps, 1951–52) and **JW** (0 caps, 1965)

A third brother, Koos, was a Junior Springbok.

Barnard, JH (5 caps, 1965) and **RW** (1 cap, 1969–71)

McCallum, ID (11 caps, 1970–74) and **RJ** (1 cap, 1974)

Played together in the 1st test against the British Isles in 1974

Snyman, DSL (10 caps, 1971–77) and **JCP** (3 caps, 1974)

Played together in the 2nd test against the British Isles in 1974 when Dawie came on as a substitute for Ian McCallum. Dawie played only five minutes before he had to leave the field due to an injury and was replaced by Leon Vogel.

Fourie, TT (1 cap, 1974) and **C** (4 caps, 1974–75)
Played together in three tour matches on the tour to France in 1974
Cockrell, CH (3 caps, 1969–70) and **RJ** (11 caps, 1974–81)
Jansen, JS (10 caps, 1970–72) and **E** (1 cap, 1980–81)
Botha, HE (28 caps, 1980–92) and **DS** (1 cap, 1981)
Played together in the 1st test against New Zealand in 1981. Also played together in two tour matches in New Zealand and USA in 1981.
Visagie, PJ (25 caps, 1967–71) and **GP** (0 caps, 1981)
Muller, HL (2 caps, 1986–94) and **PG** (33 caps, 1992–99)
They were on the same tour in 1994 but never played together in a match.
Rossouw, PWG (43 caps, 1997–2000) and **C** (0 caps, 2000)
They were on the same tour in 2000 but never played together in a match.
Cronjé, G (3 caps, 2003–04) and **J** (32 caps, 2004–07)
Played together in two test matches, against Ireland and Wales, in 2004.
Du Plessis, JN (24 caps, 2007–10) and **BW** (36 caps, 2007–10)
Played together in five test matches. One test against New Zealand in 2007 and four in 2010 (Ireland, Wales, Scotland & England).
Ndungane, AZ (11 caps, 2006–07) and **OM** (7 caps, 2008–10)
The first twins to play for South Africa. They are identical twins who both play on the right wing.

Two brothers and a son/nephew
Walker, Henry (1910) and **Alf** (1921–24) with **Harry** (1953–56), son of Alf.

— SPRINGBOK SONS-IN-LAW —

Arthur Williams, who played in the first test against the British Isles in 1910, appeared in this test match together with Archie Marsberg who was to become his son-in-law. Williams in fact acquired another rugby Springbok as a son-in-law when a second daughter married Bert Kipling, the 1931–33 Springbok.

Ryk van Schoor, the big-tackling centre from 1949 to 1953, married the daughter of Theuns Kruger, the 1921–28 Springbok hooker.

— SPRINGBOK UNCLES AND NEPHEWS —

Jan Lotz was the son of **Phil Mostert's** sister.
Felix du Plessis was the son of **Nic du Plessis's** brother.
George Daneel was the son of **Henry Daneel's** brother.
Bertus van der Merwe was the son of **Alvi van der Merwe's** brother.
Johnny Bester was the son of **Jack Bester's** brother.
Jacques Olivier is the son of **Jan Ellis's** sister.
Ryk van Schoor is the son of **George van Reenen's** sister.
Chris Koch is the son of **George van Reenen's** sister.
Chester Williams is the son of **Avril Williams'** brother.
Ray Mordt is the son of **Roger Sheriff's** sister.
Gert Brynard's wife **Rhoda** (née Howe) was a niece of **PeeWee Howe.**

— SPRINGBOK COUSINS —

Boy de Villiers and the brothers **Japie** and **Willie Krige.**
'Koei' Brink and **John Botha.**
'Mary' Jackson and **'Patats' Cloete.**
Wally Mills and **Louis Louw.**
Boy Morkel was a cousin of the brothers **Gerhard** and **Jackie.**
Dougie Morkel was also a cousin of the brothers **Gerhard** and **Jackie.**
Louis Babrow and **Morris Zimerman.**
Flappie and **Butch Lochner.**

— SPRINGBOK BROTHERS-IN-LAW —

HH Castens was married to **Edward Little's** sister.
Dick Lockyear was married to **Ian Kirkpatrick's** sister.
Nick Mallett is married to **Peter Whipp's** sister.
Drikus Hattingh is married to **Ruben Kruger's** sister.
Rudolf Straeuli is married to **Johan Roux's** sister.
Dick Muir is married to **Russell Bennett's** sister.

— SPRINGBOKS WHO MARRIED SISTERS —

Louis Strydom and **Jorrie Jordaan** are married to two sisters.
Tonie Roux and **Piet du Plessis** are married to two sisters.
Marius Hurter and **Heinrich Rodgers** are married to two sisters.

— SPRINGBOK GRANDFATHER AND GRANDSON —

Jan Pickard and **Francois Louw**.

— CRONJÉ – THE LUCKY UNLUCKIEST SPRINGBOK? —

Kerneels Cronjé, wing of Eastern Transvaal on the 1965 Springbok tour to Australia and New Zealand, could count himself as both one of the luckiest and unluckiest players to appear in the register of Springbok rugby players.

Cronjé was lucky in that he is the only Springbok in 118 years to have played in an unofficial game only, while still getting his Springbok cap.

The South African Rugby Union (and its predecessors) have a rule that Springboks who are selected for an overseas tour or tournament and who leave South African shores on such tour are automatically capped, irrespective of whether they actually ever appear in a Springbok jersey on such an overseas tour.

In many other respects Cronjé could lay claim to be the unluckiest Springbok ever, or, as he light-heartedly refers to himself: the 'nearly-there man'.

On the 1965 Springbok tour Cronjé was selected for the first game against a Western Australian XV in Perth. This was an unofficial game and the points scored and records set in this game do not form part of the Springbok statistical history. Cronjé made a brilliant debut for the Boks, scoring two tries in his team's 102–0 victory. In this match he pulled his hamstring. At the time it was thought that the injury was not serious, and on the basis of his performance in Perth, Cronjé was informed by the tour management that he would play in the first test against Australia in Sydney on 19 June 1965.

Alas, the injury never healed, and halfway through the tour Cronjé decided to return to South Africa. A test cap (and a debut appearance for the Springboks in an official match) for Cronjé was so near, yet so far. That injury also signalled the end of his rugby career.

A less-known fact is that Cronjé nearly gained international colours in a second sport: athletics. Because of an ankle injury, Cronjé, a 440 yards specialist, missed out on selection as a member of the 1960 Springbok team to the Olympic Games in Rome, the last Games with South African participation before the country was isolated for nearly

30 years because of the National Party's policy of racial segregation.

After leaving the South African Air Force, Cronjé became a commercial pilot with South African Airways (SAA), but in 1975, at the age of 45, his professional career as a pilot was cut short when he was diagnosed with Parkinson's disease. This happened shortly before he would have been promoted to the rank of flight captain on SAA's overseas fleet. In those days SAA aircraft still sported a Springbok emblem on their tail, and SAA craft were generally referred to as 'Springboks'. SAA's emergency code-call was also 'Springbok'. In an ironic twist of fate Cronjé was once again denied the opportunity to become a 'flying Springbok', and for the third time in his life he became known as the 'nearly-there man'.

— CAPPED BUT UNPLAYED —

Faan Conradie (1965) and Gus Theron (2003) took the term lucky (or perhaps rather: 'unlucky') one step further when they were capped without ever donning a Springbok jersey in an official or unofficial game.

On the 1965 tour to Ireland and Scotland in 1965, Keith Oxlee and Jannie Barnard were the two flyhalves. Oxlee only played in the first game on tour against a Combined Provinces XV but was injured. Faan Conradie was called up as a replacement but never actually appeared in any of the games, and was never selected again. Gus Theron was a member of the 2003 Tri-Nations squad in Australia and New Zealand. He was injured before appearing in any match.

— HAPPY AT HOME —

The Springboks have played tests at 19 grounds in South Africa.

Venue	First Use (Opps)	P	W	D	L
Port Elizabeth (Crusader Ground)	30 Jul 1891 (GB)	10	6	1	3
Kimberley (Eclectic CG)	29 Aug 1891 (GB)	1	–	–	1
Cape Town (Newlands)	5 Sep 1891 (GB)	48	32	2	14
Johannesburg (Old Wanderers)	22 Aug 1896 (GB)	4	2	1	1
Kimberley (Athletic Club)	29 Aug 1896 (GB)	2	–	1	1
Durban (Kingsmead)	16 Aug 1924 (GB)	5	4	–	1

Johannesburg (Ellis Park)	21 Jul 1928 (NZ)	43	30	2	11
Bloemfontein (Springbok Park)	2 Sep 1933 (Aus)	1	–	–	1
Pretoria (Loftus Versfeld)	3 Sep 1955 (BI)	30	22	–	8
Port Elizabeth (Boet Erasmus)	30 Apr 1960 (Sco)	16	14	1	1
Bloemfontein (Free State)	13 Aug 1960 (NZ)	18	13	1	4
Durban (King's Park)	21 Jul 1962 (BI)	26	16	3	7
Johannesburg (New Wanderers)	26 Apr 1980 (Sam)	1	1	–	–
Springs (PAM Brink)	25 Jul 1964 (Fra)	2	1	–	1
East London (Waverley/Absa)	10 Jun 2000 (Can)	2	2	–	–
East London (ABSA Stadium)	11 Jun 2005 (Uru)	1	1	–	–
Rustenberg (Royal Bafokeng)	2 Sep 2006 (NZ)	1	1	–	–
Puma Stadium (Witbank)	19 Jun 2010	1	1	–	–
FNB Stadium (Soweto)	21 August 2010	1	0	–	1

In addition, two further grounds in South Africa hosted matches during the 1995 Rugby World Cup, but neither featured the home nation:

Rustenberg (Olympia Park)	France 54, Cote d'Ivoire 18 (30 May 1995)
	Tonga 29, Cote d'Ivoire 11 (3 June 1995)
	Scotland 89, Cote d'Ivoire 0 (26 May 1995)
Stellenbosch (Danie Craven Stadium)	Australia 42, Romania 3 (3 June 1995)

— ELS SPRINGS A LEAK —

In 1981, Jannie Els, the hard-running Eastern Transvaal centre, became a tragic victim of the 'Press leaks' controversy which hit South African rugby. Els, who went to the Springbok trials as a late replacement and wound up playing centre in the A team in the second half of the main trial, was told that he had been picked for the Springbok team to meet the Irish in the first test at Newlands. The news was conveyed to him by Eastern Transvaal secretary Ben Erwee following a call from a Johannesburg morning newspaper. The reporter claimed that he had the

Springbok team on good authority and that Els had made it. But when the team was announced late on Saturday night, Els' name was missing.

Dr Danie Craven, the President of the SA Rugby Board, later said: 'Telling Jannie Els that he was not in the Springbok team is one of the saddest things I have heard of. What a thing to do to any man.'

The truth behind the whole unfortunate tale will probably never surface, and even if it does, it will provide little consolation for Els.

— THE UNLUCKY ONES —

Apart from Jannie Els, the history of Springbok rugby is resplendent with more players who were selected but not capped:

John Cecil ('Daddy') Carden of Eastern Province was selected to represent South Africa at the Crusaders Ground, Port Elizabeth in the very first test against the first British touring side in 1891 on 30 July, but was stricken with typhoid fever, and never got another chance. Carden, at the age of only nineteen, captained Eastern Province in the first SA Board tournament at Kimberley in 1889. When Paul Roos's Springbok team toured the United Kingdom in 1906, the SA Rugby Board picked Louis Smuts, then president of the Western Province Rugby Union, as manager. However, he was unable to accept due to business reasons, and Carden took his place as manager with distinction.

John Robert Adolph de Melker of Griquas played against the British Isles for his province on 20 July 1891. He was selected to play halfback for South Africa against the British Isles in the second test at Kimberley on 29 August 1891. Three days earlier he was also chosen to play against the British for the Cape Colony team, also in Kimberley, but could not play in either match due to an injury. His brother Syd played two tests for South Africa, one in 1903 against the British Isles and one in 1906 against England on the tour to the United Kingdom.

HR Eaton of Eastern Province was chosen to represent South Africa in the first test against the British Isles in 1896 at the Crusaders Ground in Port Elizabeth, but had to withdraw due to injury.

Tom van Renen, a brother of Charlie (1891–96) and Willie (1903) was chosen for the fourth test in 1896 against the British Isles at Newlands, Cape Town, but he had to withdraw because of injury.

Sydney Heatlie, a brother of Fairy Heatlie (1891–1903), was chosen for the third test against the British Isles in 1903 at Newlands, Cape Town, but had to withdraw because of injury.

Frank Maxwell of Transvaal was selected to play wing for South Africa against the British Isles in the second test at the Old Wanderers in

Johannesburg on 22 August 1896. At the last minute he had to withdraw because of an injury and it was decided to replace him with the Griqualand West fullback Theo Samuels. Samuels scored two tries (the first two tries ever scored by South Africa) and Maxwell was never chosen again.

Bertie Mosenthal, a Transvaal forward, was selected for the 1906–07 tour to Britain. He withdrew from the team at the last minute and was replaced by Billy Millar, who became South Africa's captain in 1910.

Leon Barnard, a wing from South Western Districts, was chosen for South Africa against the Wallabies in the first test at Newlands in 1933. On his way to Cape Town he developed a painful boil on the knee. He was replaced by the 19-year-old Freddy Turner and was never chosen again. Turner played for South Africa until 1938. Turner was flown down from Port Elizabeth to Cape Town for the test, the first Springbok to make use of a form of transport which was then still in its infancy.

In 1973, following the cancellation of the tour by New Zealand to South Africa, the selectors decided to hold trials in preparation for the British Lions tour that lay ahead in 1974. After the trials a South Africa XV team was chosen that played two games, against Western Province and Northern Transvaal, and wore white jerseys. From this 'touring' team the following players never became Springboks: **Frans Oeschger** (WP), **Pierre Spies** (Northern Transvaal – father of current Springbok also called Pierre), **Grahame Thorne** (Natal – the 1970 All Black centre who later emigrated to South Africa), **Buddy Swartz** (Griqualand West), **Pikkie du Toit** (Free State), **Gert Schutte** (Griqualand West), **Hendré Reyneke** (Boland), **André Lötter** (Northern Transvaal), **Johnny Joubert** (Boland), **Jan Tromp** (Western Transvaal – the father of future Springbok Henry).

In 1985, following the cancellation of the tour by New Zealand to South Africa, the South African selectors chose a 'Springbok' team that went on an internal tour and played four matches, against a Transvaal Barbarians side, a Cape Barbarians side, a Central Barbarians side and a South African Barbarians, and on each occasion wore proper Springbok jerseys. Five players who went on this tour but were destined never to become Springboks: **Calla Scholtz** (WP), **Dolly Ntaka** (SA Rugby Association), **Wilfred Cupido** (WP League), **John Robbie** (Transvaal) and **Wessel Lightfoot** (Free State).

Jan Lock, the Northern Transvaal tighthead prop, was chosen for the first test against the World XV at Newlands in 1989, but had to withdraw because of injury. He was replaced by Flippie van der Merwe, who gained his sixth and last Springbok cap.

On 12 October 1991 in Durban the South African season ended with a match between the 'Springboks' and the Junior Springboks, with the main team wearing full Springbok jerseys. Interestingly, Michael du

Plessis was the Springbok captain, although Naas Botha was also in the team. All the players who played for the 'Springboks' were either already capped or went on to be capped, with the exception of Stef Nel. The Western Province scrumhalf sat on the bench but did not get on the field. Tragically Nel died in a car crash in 1993 along with team mate and halfback partner Cameron Oliver. (Nel was playing for Transvaal at that stage.) Gerbrand Grobler, who played fullback for the Junior Springboks that day in 1991, also lost his life in a car crash three years later. Grobler remains the only player to represent his province in a Currie Cup final in both rugby and cricket.

— FORTUNATE VAN BROEKHUIZEN —

Just prior to the fourth and final test of the 1896 series at Newlands in Cape Town on 5 September, JJ 'Scraps' Wessels, the Western Province forward who played in the first three tests, had to withdraw because of an injury. He was replaced by the University of Stellenbosch (Maties) forward Herman van Broekhuizen, who played in his only test. Van Broekhuizen never played for Western Province, making him the only Springbok never to appear for any province.

— INTERNATIONAL RUGBY BEFORE PROVINCIAL RUGBY —

Player	SA debut	Provincial debut
Wally Mills	27 August 1910	6 September 1910 (WP)
Bai Wrentmore	10 October 1912	11 September 1919 (WP)
PK Albertyn	16 August 1924	16 September 1924 (SWD)
JC van der Westhuizen	18 August 1928	25 August 1928 (WP)
Danie Craven	10 October 1931	31 May 1932 (WP)
Johnny Bester	12 June 1937	16 April 1938 (WP)
Dawie Snyman	26 June 1971	14 August 1971 (WP)

— LOUBSER TURNS DOWN A CAP —

Bob Loubser, the University of Stellenbosch and Western Province wing, was chosen for the first test against the British Isles in Johannesburg on 26 August 1903, but on the advice of his future father-in-law, Dr JH Neethling, did not accept. Dr Neethling felt he was too young for international rugby and that he risked injury if he played on the hard Old Wanderers ground, which then had a gravel surface. Loubser made his debut later in the series in the third and final test.

— KRIGE WANTS THE BALL —

Japie Krige, one of South Africa's first rugby heroes, made his debut at centre in the first test against the British Isles at Johannesburg in 1903. It did not turn out a happy international debut for Krige: as a centre he liked plenty of work, but the Griqualand West pair of half-backs, 'Uncle' Dobbin and Jackie Powell, rather kept the ball to themselves. Krige then declined the invitation to play in the second test at Kimberley because 'Dobbin and Powell won't let me see the ball'. Krige played in the third test after the selectors, Barry Heatlie (who was the captain), Percy Jones and Biddy Anderson, replaced Dobbin and Powell, thereby making sure Krige would be happy.

— ASHLEY'S TRAM TRIP —

Syd Ashley from Western Province, who played centre in the second test against the British Isles in 1903 in Kimberley, was originally chosen to partner Japie Krige in the centre for the third test in 1903 at Newlands in Cape Town, but then unfortunately injured himself when he got off a tram a few days before the match. Ashley never played for South Africa again. He later moved to Rhodesia and skippered his new side in 1914 at the Currie Cup tournament in Durban and Pietermaritzburg.

— LIKE FATHER, LIKE SON —

The shortest gap between a father gaining his final cap for South Africa and his son making his debut is just 17 years in the case of Schalk Burger senior and junior. Schalk Willem Petrus Burger senior gained the last of his six Springbok caps against the New Zealand Cavaliers at

Ellis Park, Johannesburg on 31 May 1986. At the time his son, Schalk Willem Petrus Burger junior, was aged 3. Burger junior went on to be capped at full test level against Georgia at Sydney on 24 October 2003 during the Rugby World Cup, aged just 20.

Fathers and sons who have played for South Africa:

Father	Caps	Son	Caps
Alf Walker (1921–24)	6	Harry Walker (1953–56)	4
Cecil Jennings (1937)	1	Mike Jennings (1969–70)	0
Felix du Plessis (1949)*	3	Morné du Plessis (1971–80)*	22
Mauritz van den Berg (1937)	4	Derek van den Berg (1974–76)	4
Louis Schmidt (1958–62)	2	Uli Schmidt (1986–94)	17
Joggie Viljoen (1971–72)	6	Joggie Viljoen (1996)	0
Moaner van Heerden (1974–80)	17	Wikus van Heerden (2003–07)	14
Schalk Burger (Snr) (1984–86)	6	Schalk Burger (Jnr) (2003–10)	63
Gysie Pienaar (1980–81)	13	Ruan Pienaar (2006–10)	47
Hennie Bekker (1981)	2	Andries Bekker (2008–10)	24
Flippie van der Merwe (1981–1989)	6	Flip van der Merwe (2010)	10

* Felix and Morné du Plessis are the only father and son combination to have both captained South Africa.

— RELATIVE SPORTSMEN AND -WOMEN —

Many Springboks had family connections with successful international sportsmen and -women:

AR Richards (3 caps, 1891): brother Dicky played one cricket test for South Africa against England at Cape Town in 1888–89, scoring 0 and 4.

WM Bissett (2 caps, 1891): brother Murray played three cricket tests for South Africa between 1899 and 1910 with a top score of 35.

WS Taberer (1 cap, 1896): brother Henry captained SA in his only cricket test, against Australia at the Old Wanderers in Johannesburg (the same venue as Bill's only rugby cap six years later), scoring 2 and taking one wicket.

FTD Aston (4 caps, 1896): brother Randolph was the crack centre of Bill MacLagan's Great Britain touring team five years earlier, scoring tries in the 1st and 3rd tests.

WMC McEwan (16 caps for Scotland 1894-1900 and two for SA in 1903): brother Matthew McEwan was also a Scottish International, gaining 15 caps between 1886 and 1892.

Syd Ashley (1 cap, 1903): brother WH 'Gobo' played cricket for South Africa against England at Cape Town in 1889, scoring 1 and 0 and taking seven wickets for 95 in his only innings.

RCB van Ryneveld (2 caps, 1910): his son Clive played rugby for England in 1949 (4 caps, 3 tries) and played for the SA cricket team in 19 tests from 1951 to 1958, scoring 724 runs at 26,81 and taking 17 wickets at 39,47. Clive was captain in 8 tests between 1956 and 1958.

HPK de Jongh (1 cap, 1928): his son Ian became a Springbok athlete in 1950.

JA Krige, a brother of JD (5 caps, 1903–06) and WA (0 caps, 1912), played for England against Wales at Swansea in 1920 while studying at the famous Guy's Hospital in London.

DA Macdonald (1 cap, 1974): brother of DSM Macdonald who played seven tests for Scotland from 1977 to 1978.

PJ Spies (19 caps, 2006–08): father Pierre Spies (Snr) was a Springbok in Athletics, competing in the 110 m hurdles.

HSV Muller (13 caps, 1949–53): daughter Melanie played hockey for South Africa.

BS van der Merwe (1 cap 1949): son Marius played baseball for South Africa.

F du T Roux (27 caps, 1960–70): son Pietie gained Springbok colours in Athletics, competing in the pole vault.

JT Small (47 caps, 1992–1997): father V Small played football for South Africa.

— CRICKETERS AGAINST TOURISTS —

Eight Springbok test cricketers have played rugby against touring teams to South Africa:

Aubrey Faulkner (Witwatersrand against the British Isles in 1903): 25 cricket caps for South Africa between 1906 and 1924, scoring 1 754 runs at 40,79 with a top score of 204, and taking 82 wickets at 26,58.

Herbie Taylor (Natal against British Isles in 1910): 42 crickets caps for South Africa between 1912 and 1932, scoring 2 936 runs at 40,77 with a top score of 176, and taking 5 wickets.

Jack Siedle (Natal against New Zealand 1928): 18 cricket caps for South Africa, scoring 977 runs at 28,73 with a top score of 141, and taking one wicket.

Koos Duminy (Combined Pretoria against New Zealand 1928): 3 cricket caps for the Springboks between 1927 and 1929, scoring 30 runs and taking one wicket.
Roy McLean (Natal against Australia 1953): 40 cricket caps for South Africa between 1951 and 1964, scoring 2 120 runs at 30,28 with a top score of 142.
Eddie Barlow (Transvaal against New Zealand 1960): 30 cricket caps for South Africa between 1961 and 1970, scoring 2 516 runs at 45,74 with a top score of 201, and taking 40 wickets at 34,05.
Peter Carlstein (Western Transvaal against Ireland 1960): 8 cricket caps for South Africa between 1958 and 1964, scoring 190 runs at 14,61.
Peter Kirsten (Quaggas against British Lions 1974): 12 cricket caps and 40 one-day internationals for South Africa between 1991 and 1994.
Also One-Day International player:
Errol Stewart (Natal against British and Irish Lions 1997, bench DNP): six one-day internationals for South Africa between 1993 and 2002, scoring 61 runs at 15,25.

— SPRINGBOKS IN THE FAMILY —

The Bekkers – Jaap, Dolf and Martiens (all played test rugby for South Africa). A fourth brother, Daan, was a Springbok boxer who won the heavyweight bronze medal at the Melbourne Olympic Games in 1956, losing to eventual gold medallist Pete Rademacher of the USA in the semi-finals. Four years later in Rome he won the silver medal, losing to Italian Franco de Piccoli in the final. Their sister Corrie was a Springbok athlete in 1959.
The Du Plessis' – Felix (1949) and Morné (1971–80) both captained the Springboks in rugby. Felix's wife Pat (née Smethurst) captained South Africa in hockey. Her brother Horace Smethurst captained the SA Soccer team. Felix was also a nephew of 1921 Springbok Nic du Plessis.
The Kirkpatricks – Eva Kirkpatrick was a Springbok hockey player from 1925 to 1930. Her son Ian Kirkpatrick played flyhalf and centre for South Africa in 13 tests from 1953 to 1961. His wife Norma and his sister Rhona played hockey for South Africa. Rhona was married to Springbok scrumhalf Dick Lockyear who played six tests for South Africa from 1960 to 1961.
The Nels – Lofty Nel, who played eleven tests for South Africa from 1960 to 1970, is married to Hester, who played jukskei for South Africa. Her two sisters, San Beukes and Dina Dreyer, also played jukskei for South Africa, as did their mother Dina Muller. Lofty and Hester's son

Pieter played rugby for the South Africa Schools in 1983 and was a centre for Northern Transvaal.

— DUAL RUGBY UNION INTERNATIONALS —

Capped for South Africa and another country	
Alex Frew	South Africa (1, 1903) and Scotland (3, 1901)
Willie McEwan	South Africa (2, 1903) and Scotland (16, 1894–1903)
Hugh Ferris	South Africa (1, 1903) and Ireland (4, 1900–01)
Barry Heatlie	South Africa (6, 1891–1903) and Argentina (1, 1910)
Frank Mellish	South Africa (6, 1921–24) and England (6, 1920–21)
Jack Gage	South Africa (1, 1933) and Ireland (4, 1926–27)
Tiaan Strauss	South Africa (15, 1992–94) and Australia (11, 1999)
John Allan	South Africa (13, 1993–96) and Scotland (9, 1990–91)
Adrian Garvey	South Africa (28, 1996–99) and Zimbabwe (25, 1988–93)
Christian Stewart	South Africa (3, 1998) and Canada (14, 1991–95)

— SPRINGBOK LEGENDS: HENNIE MULLER —

Hendrik Scholtz Vosloo (Hennie) Muller hit the international scene in 1949 like a bomb. The two New Zealand scrumhalves Bill Conrad and Larry Savage were both split-seconds too slow in serving the flyhalf Jim Kearney. This opened the way for the Springboks, guided by their coach and national selector Danie Craven, to use Hennie Muller to nullify all their opponent's efforts to mount constructive attacks. There is no doubt that at his peak Hennie Muller was one of the fastest forwards ever to wear the Springbok jersey. In addition he could tackle with frightening ferocity and he was a complete master of all the basics of the game. He was also always superbly fit, and if ever a player had the 'killer instinct', it was the lean, almost gaunt Springbok so aptly named 'Die Windhond' ('The Greyhound') by Craven. Craven turned him into a one-man demolition squad to seek and destroy the All Black halves and three-quarters. The instant the ball left the scrum or the lineout, Muller would swoop down on the flyhalf, and if he should by some miracle manage to get the ball to the centres, Muller's exceptional pace would enable him to arrive virtually simultaneously with the ball.

'I would unhesitatingly say that Hennie Muller was the greatest loose-forward I have ever seen,' wrote Bob Scott, the greatest fullback of his time, in his biography. 'He was the complete footballer and he, more than anybody, determined the results of the tests.'

The Springboks won all four their tests against New Zealand in 1949.

In 1951 Hennie Muller was chosen as vice-captain of the tour to the United Kingdom and France. When the tour captain, Basil Kenyon, sustained an eye injury early on during the tour and had to undergo an operation, Muller took over as captain in all five winning tests on tour. In 1953 Muller captained South Africa in all four tests against the touring Wallaby side. South Africa won three of the four tests, losing only the second test 14–18 at Newlands, Muller's only loss in 13 test matches that he played in.

HENNIE MULLER FACTFILE
Born: 26 March 1922 in Witbank, Eastern Transvaal
Provinces: Transvaal, Western Province
Caps: 13 (W12, D0, L1)
Scoring: 16 points (3 tries, 2 conversions and 1 penalty)
Springbok debut: vs New Zealand on 16 July 1949

Hennie Muller is ready to put pressure on the opponent's backline.

— FORTY-SIX IN A ROW —

John Smit holds the record for the most consecutive appearances for South Africa, with 46 from 2003 to 2007, including 44 as the starting hooker – the record for the most successive tests started.

Ollie le Roux played in 25 successive tests between 1998 and 1999 but started just 3 of them – the other 22 were all as a replacement!

Syd Nomis played his entire 5-year, 25-test Springbok career in successive matches, the first three at centre and the next 22 on the wing.

Caps	Name	From	To	Notes
46	John Smit	11 Oct 2003	16 Jun 2007	2 rep
39	Gary Teichmann	2 Jul 1996	12 Jun 1999	
28	Victor Matfield	7 June 2008	19 June 2010	2 rep

26	André Snyman	15 Dec 1996	5 Dec 1998	1 rep
26	André Vos	24 Oct 1999	1 Dec 2001**	Last 26 caps (2 reps)
25	Syd Nomis	12 Aug 1967*	3 Jun 1972**	Complete career
25	André Venter	8 Nov 1997	3 Oct 1999	5 reps
25	Ollie le Roux	13 Jun 1998	4 Nov 1999	22 reps

* Test debut

** Last test appearance

— GETTING THE FULL MONTY —

Percy Montgomery became the first Springbok to play 100 test matches for South Africa when he appeared against New Zealand in a Tri-Nations game at Newlands, Cape Town on 16 August 2008. He extended this record to 102 on 30 August 2008 against Australia at Coca-Cola Park (previously Ellis Park) before he decided to retire from international rugby. Montgomery's career started way back in 1997 against the British and Irish Lions in the second test match at King's Park in Durban on 28 June, 1977. John Smit became the second Springbok to play in 100 test matches, against New Zealand on 21 August 2010 at the FNB Stadium in Soweto. A week later, on 28 August 2010, Victor Matfield became the third Springbok to reach this milestone, against Australia at his homeground, Loftus Versfeld.

The top appearances in Springbok rugby are:

No	Name	Career	Caps	Starts+Rep
1	Victor Matfield	2001–2010	105	100+5
2	Percy Montgomery	1997–2008	102	90+12
	John Smit	2000–2010	102	87+15
4	Joost van der Westhuizen	1993–2003	89	78+11
5	Os du Randt	1994–2007	80	75+5
6	Mark Andrews	1994–2001	77	74+3

— FIFTY UP —

Mark Andrews was the first Springbok player to reach 50 caps. Having made his debut against England at Newlands on 11 June 1994, he reached the milestone against Wales on 14 November 1998 at the Wembley Stadium in London.

Here are the 15 players who have reached a half-century of caps and the occasion on which they achieved the feat.

Player	Opponent (Venue)	50th Cap date	
Mark Andrews	v Wales (Wembley Stadium)	14 Nov 1998	
Joost van der Westhuizen	v England (Twickenham)	5 Dec 1998	
André Venter	v Australia (Sydney)	29 Jul 2000	
Percy Montgomery	v Italy (Genoa)	17 Nov 2001	replacement
Ollie le Roux	v Argentina (Springs)	29 Jun 2002	
Breyton Paulse	v Ireland (Dublin)	13 Nov 2004	
Os du Randt	v England (Twickenham)	20 Nov 2004	
John Smit	v Wales (Cardiff)	19 Nov 2005	captain
Victor Matfield	v New Zealand (Wellington)	22 Jul 2006	
Bakkies Botha	v New Zealand (Dunedin)	12 Jul 2007	
Albert van den Berg	v USA (Montpellier)	30 Sep 2007	
CJ van der Linde	v Italy (Cape Town)	21 Jun 2008	
Joe van Niekerk	v Argentina (Johannesburg)	9 Aug 2008	two tries
Juan Smith	v New Zealand (Cape Town)	16 Aug 2008	
Schalk Burger	v British and Irish Lions (Pretoria)	27 June 2009	

— CHANGING TRY VALUES —

The value of a try has gradually increased over the years from one point to the modern-day value of five, which was first introduced in 1992.

The following table lists the Springbok player who had the honour of scoring his country's first try at the new try value, and the last try scored using an old value.

Value	Date	First try	Date	Last try
1 point	no one-point try scored by South Africa			
2 points	did not play a test with two points for a try			
3 points	22 Aug 1896	Theo Samuels	7 Aug 1971	Jan Ellis
4 points	27 Jul 1974	Peter Cronjé	2 Sep 1989	Michael du Plessis
5 points	15 Aug 1992	Danie Gerber		

— TOP TRYERS —

Joost van der Westhuizen scored the most tries for the Springboks in his test career with 38 test tries in his 89 appearances. Bryan Habana, the speedy winger, has now equalled Van der Westhuizen's record, having scored 38 test tries in his 68 tests.

The following is a list of the players with the most test tries in a career:

Tries	Player	Tests	Starts+Rep	Career
38	Joost van der Westhuizen	89	78+11	1993–2003
38	Bryan Habana	68	66+2	2004–10
30	Jaque Fourie	62	49+13	2003–10
26	Breyton Paulse	64	58+6	1999–2007
25	Percy Montgomery	102	90+12	1997–2008
21	Pieter Rossouw	43	39+4	1997–2003
20	James Small	47	43+4	1992–97
19	Danie Gerber	24	24	1980–92
19	Stefan Terblanche	37	32+5	1998–2003
19	Jean de Villiers	67	64+3	2002–10
14	Chester Williams	27	20+7	1993–2000

— POINTS MACHINES —

Percy Montgomery has scored by far the most points for South Africa in his test career with his 893 points in 102 tests.

Highest scorers of most points in a test career are:

Points	Player	Tests	T	C	P	D	Career
893	Percy Montgomery	102	25	153	148	6	1997–2008
322	Morné Steyn	25	4	37	71	5	2009–10
312	Naas Botha	28	2	50	50	18	1980–92
240	Joel Stransky	22	6	30	47	3	1993–96
221	Braam van Straaten	21	2	23	55	–	1999–2001
190	Joost van der Westhuizen	89	38	–	–	–	1993–2003
190	Bryan Habana	68	38	–	–	–	2004–10
181	Jannie de Beer	13	2	33	27	8	1997–99
171	André Pretorius	31	2	31	25	8	2002–07
156	Henry Honiball	35	1	38	25	–	1993–99
150	Jaque Fourie	62	30	–	–	–	2003–10
148	Butch James	35	3	26	26	1	2001–10
145	Louis Koen	15	–	23	31	2	2000–03

— STRIKING OUT —

Danie Gerber still has the best strike rate in terms of scoring tries per test with his 19 test tries in 24 test matches. Bryan Habana, who is in sixth place with his 38 test tries in 68 test matches, can still overtake Gerber in the future.

Players who have scored a try every two games or better and have played at least ten tests are:

%	Player	Tries	Tests	Career
79,2	Danie Gerber	19	24	1980–92
66,7	Ray Mordt	12	18	1980–84
60,0	Basie van Wyk	6	10	1951–55

60,0	Hennie van Zyl	6	10	1960–61
60,0	Gerrie Germishuys	12	20	1974–81
55,9	Bryan Habana	38	68	2004–10
51,9	Chester Williams	14	27	1993–2000
51,4	Stefan Terblanche	19	37	1998–03

— A TRY EVERY 140 PLAYING MINUTES OR BETTER —

Danie Gerber averaged a try for every 101,1 minutes that he played on the pitch.

Here is the list of the best strike rates for those who have played in at least ten tests:

Try/Min	Player	Tries	Tests	Career
101,1	Danie Gerber	19	24	1980–92
117,5	Chester Williams	14	27	1993–2000
119,3	Brent Russell	8	23	2002–06
120,0	Ray Mordt	12	18	1980–84
129,8	Bryan Habana	38	68	2004–10
132,4	Gaffie du Toit	5	14	1998–2006
132,9	Stefan Terblanche	19	37	1998–2003
133,3	Gerrie Germishuys	12	20	1974–81
133,3	Basie van Wyk	6	10	1951–55
133,3	Hennie van Zyl	6	10	1960–61
137,8	Jaque Fourie	30	62	2003–10

— PROLIFIC BOKS —

Jannie de Beer, the Free State flyhalf, has the highest average of test points per test with 13,92. Morné Steyn with 12,88, Naas Botha with 11,14, Joel Stransky with 10,91 and Braam van Straaten with 10,52 are the only other players who averaged more than 10 points per game.

The list of the best accumulators for those who have played in at least ten tests is:

Pts per Test	Player	Points	Tests	Career
13,92	Jannie de Beer	181	13	1997–99
12,88	Morné Steyn	322	25	2009–10
11,14	Naas Botha	312	28	1980–92
10,91	Joel Stransky	240	22	1993–96
10,52	Braam van Straaten	221	21	1999–2001
9,67	Louis Koen	145	15	2000–03
8,75	Percy Montgomery	893	102	1997–2008
7,71	Gaffie du Toit	108	14	1998–2006
5,64	Ian McCallum	62	11	1970–74
5,52	André Pretorius	171	31	2002–07
5,20	Piet Visagie	130	25	1967–71

— FAST SCORERS —

Jannie de Beer is the only Springbok to have scored points at a rate of better than one for every five minutes played, with his point for every 4 minutes 57 seconds of playing time.

The list of fast scorers who have gained at least ten caps is:

Mins a Pt	Name	Points	Tests	Career
4' 57"	Jannie de Beer	181	13	1997–99
5' 06"	Morné Steyn	322	25	2009–10
6' 08"	Gaffie du Toit	108	14	1998–2006
6' 20"	Braam van Straaten	221	21	1999–2001
6' 28"	Joel Stransky	240	22	1993–96
7' 04"	Louis Koen	145	15	2000–03
7' 09"	Naas Botha	312	28	1980–92
8' 01"	Percy Montgomery	893	102	1997–2008

— SEVENTY UP —

The Springboks scored 100 points in a test for the first time in 1999 against a hapless Italian side. In 2005 the Springboks posted their biggest ever score against Uruguay with their 134–3 victory, Tonderai Chavhanga scoring six tries on debut – a new South African record.

The highest test scores are:

Total	Date	Opponent	Result	Venue
134	11 Jun 2005	Uruguay	134–3	East London
105	15 Aug 2007	Namibia	105–13	Cape Town
101	19 Jun 1999	Italy	101–0	Durban
96	27 Jun 1998	Wales	96–13	Pretoria
74	12 Jun 1999	Italy	74–3	Port Elizabeth
74	10 Jun 1997	Tonga	74–10	Cape Town
72	11 Oct 2003	Uruguay	72–6	Perth

— BIG VICTORIES —

The Springboks' first victory with a margin of more than 50 points was in 1995 when they beat Samoa 60–8 at Ellis Park in preparation for the 1995 Rugby World Cup. South Africa achieved this feat on eleven more occasions, with the highest winning margin of 131 points against Uruguay in 2005.

The 50-point wins are:

Margin	Date	Opponent	Result	Venue
131	11 Jun 2005	Uruguay	134–3	East London
101	19 Jun 1999	Italy	101–0	Durban
92	15 Aug 2007	Namibia	105–13	Cape Town
83	27 Jun 1998	Wales	96–13	Pretoria
71	12 Jun 1999	Italy	74–3	Port Elizabeth
66	11 Oct 2003	Uruguay	72–6	Perth
64	10 Jun 1997	Tonga	74–10	Cape Town
58	6 Dec 1997	Scotland	68–10	Edinburgh

Margin	Date	Opponent	Result	Venue
54	9 Aug 2008	Argentina	63–9	Johannesburg
52	13 Apr 1995	Samoa	60–8	Johannesburg
52	9 Sep 2007	Samoa	59–7	Paris
50	1 Nov 2003	Samoa	60–10	Brisbane

— FORTY AGAINST —

The Springboks have conceded fifty points in a test match on only three occasions, with the 35–55 loss to New Zealand in the 1997 Tri-Nations the first of these. The Springboks then conceded fifty points against England in 2002 (3–53) and against New Zealand (16–52) in 2003.

The list of games where most points were conceded are:

Total	Date	Opponent	Result	Venue
55	9 Aug 1997	New Zealand	35–55	Auckland
53	23 Nov 2002	England	3–53	Twickenham
52	19 Jul 2003	New Zealand	16–52	Pretoria
49	15 Jul 2006	Australia	0–49	Brisbane
45	26 Aug 2006	New Zealand	26–45	Pretoria
44	8 Jul 2000	Australia	23–44	Melbourne
41	20 Jul 2002	New Zealand	20–41	Wellington
41	4 Sept 2010	Australia	39–41	Bloemfontein
40	19 Aug 2000	New Zealand	46–40	Johannesburg

— LARGE REVERSALS —

South Africa suffered their biggest loss of 50 points (3–53) against England in 2002 at Twickenham. This test will be remembered for the red card issued to lock Jannes Labuschagne early in the test.

The list of the biggest losses with margins of 20 points or over are:

Margin	Date	Opponent	Result	Venue
50	23 Nov 2002	England	3–53	Twickenham
49	15 Jul 2006	Australia	0–49	Brisbane
46	19 Jul 2003	New Zealand	16–52	Pretoria
28	10 Jul 1999	New Zealand	0–28	Dunedin
27	14 Jul 2007	New Zealand	6–33	Christchurch
26	17 Jul 1999	Australia	6–32	Brisbane
23	22 Aug 1992	Australia	3–26	Cape Town
21	8 Jul 2000	Australia	23–44	Melbourne
21	20 Jul 2002	New Zealand	20–41	Wellington
20	9 Aug 1997	New Zealand	35–55	Auckland
20	29 Jul 2000	Australia	6–26	Sydney
20	24 Nov 2001	England	9–29	Twickenham
20	9 Nov 2002	France	10–30	Marseilles
20	2 Aug 2003	Australia	9–29	Brisbane
20	8 Nov 2003	New Zealand	9–29	Melbourne
20	10 July 2010	New Zealand	12–32	Auckland

— TRIES GALORE —

The ten tries scored by South Africa against Ireland in 1912 was the record for 85 years until it was equalled against Tonga in 1997. The record was finally broken in 1999 when the Springboks scored eleven tries against Italy. Since then the Springboks have scored more than 11 tries in a test on six occasions, the record being the 21 tries scored against Uruguay in 2005.

The list of most tries in a test:
By South Africa:

Tries	Opponents	Result	Venue	Date
21	Uruguay	W 134–3	East London	11 Jun 2005
15	Italy	W 101–0	Durban	19 Jun 1999
15	Wales	W 96–13	Pretoria	27 Jun 1998
15	Namibia	W 105–13	Cape Town	15 Aug 2007
12	Uruguay	W 72–6	Perth	11 Oct 2003
12	Tonga	W 74–10	Cape Town	10 Jun 1997
11	Italy	W 74–3	Port Elizabeth	12 Jun 1999
10	Scotland	W 68–10	Edinburgh	6 Dec 1997
10	Ireland	W 38–0	Dublin	30 Nov 1912

Against:

Tries	By	Result	Venue	Date
7	New Zealand	L 35–55	Auckland	9 Aug 1997
7	England	L 3–53	Twickenham	23 Nov 2002
7	New Zealand	L 16–52	Pretoria	19 Jul 2003

— PROLIFIC DAYS —

Gerald Bosch's record of 22 points in a test match (against France in 1975) stood for 20 years until Gavin Johnson scored 28 points against Samoa in 1995. Johnson had equalled the record in 1993, as had Joel Stransky in 1994. Percy Montgomery took the record away from Johnson in 1998 with his 31 points against Wales. Jannie de Beer eclipsed Percy's mark during the 1999 Rugby World Cup against England with his 34-point haul, which included five dropped goals. Montgomery regained the record in 2007 when he scored 35 points against neighbouring Namibia.

Stirling Mortlock, the Australian centre, scored the most points against South Africa in a test, 29, in Melbourne in 2000. Four players, namely Rob Andrew, Jonny Wilkinson and Charlie Hodgson from England, along with Gerald Merceron from France, have all scored 27 points in a test match against South Africa.

For South Africa:

Pts	Player	Date	Opponent	Venue
35	Percy Montgomery	15 Aug 2007	Namibia	Cape Town
34	Jannie de Beer	24 Oct 1999	England	Paris
31	Percy Montgomery	27 Jun 1998	Wales	Pretoria
31	Morné Steyn	1 August 2010	New Zealand	Durban
30	Tonderai Chavhanga	11 Jun 2005	Uruguay	East London
29	Gaffie du Toit	12 Jun 1999	Italy	Port Elizabeth
29	Percy Montgomery	9 Sep 2007	Samoa	Paris
28	Gavin Johnson	13 Apr 1995	Samoa	Johannesburg
26	Jannie de Beer	23 Aug 1997	Australia	Pretoria
26	Percy Montgomery	06 Dec 1997	Scotland	Edinburgh
26	Morné Steyn	26 June 2010	Italy	East London
25	Joel Stransky	03 Aug 1996	Australia	Bloemfontein
25	Stefan Terblanche	19 Jun 1999	Italy	Durban

Against:

Pts	Player	Date	For	Venue
29	Stirling Mortlock	8 Jul 2000	Australia	Melbourne
27	Rob Andrew	4 Jun 1994	England	Pretoria
27	Jonny Wilkinson	24 Jun 2000	England	Bloemfontein
27	Gerald Merceron	16 Jun 2001	France	Johannesburg
27	Charlie Hodgson	20 Nov 2004	England	Twickenham
25	Carlos Spencer	9 Aug 1997	New Zealand	Auckland
25	Dan Carter	22 Jul 2006	New Zealand	Wellington

— TRY, TRY AGAIN —

Chester Williams, in 1995 against Western Samoa at the Rugby World Cup, was the first Springbok to score four tries in a test match. Pieter Rossouw equalled this record when he claimed four tries against France in 1997. Stefan Terblanche, who tallied four tries on debut against

Ireland in 1998 to equal the record, became the first player to score five tries in a test match against Italy in 1999. Tonderai Chavhanga, the Zimbabwe-born wing, scored six tries on debut against Uruguay.
For South Africa:

Tries	Player	Date	Opponent	Venue
6	Tonderai Chavhanga	11 Jun 2005	Uruguay	East London
5	Stefan Terblanche	19 Jun 1999	Italy	Durban
4	Chester Williams	10 Jun 1995	Samoa	Johannesburg
4	Pieter Rossouw	22 Nov 1997	France	Paris
4	Stefan Terblanche	13 Jun 1998	Ireland	Bloemfontein
4	Bryan Habana	9 Sep 2007	Samoa	Paris
4	Jongi Nokwe	30 Aug 2008	Australia	Johannesburg

Against:
No-one has ever managed to score a hat-trick of tries in a test against South Africa. However, there have been 30 instances of a player scoring a brace of tries in a single game. Of those Christian Cullen achieved the feat four times, while JJ Williams, Joe Rokocoko and Matt Giteau each did so twice.

— PENALTY GOALS GALORE —

Gerald Bosch's six penalties against France in 1975 was the record until 2006 when Percy Montgomery scored seven penalty goals for the Springboks on two occasions; against Scotland and France on consecutive weekends. He was joined by Morné Steyn in 2009, who scored seven penalties against Australia in 2009. Seven players, namely Gerald Bosch, Joel Stransky, Jannie de Beer, Braam van Straaten (twice), Montgomery, Louis Koen and Morné Steyn, have also scored six penalties for the Springboks in a test match.

Matt Burke from Australia and Jonny Wilkinson from England have both scored eight penalty goals in a test against South Africa.
For South Africa:

Pens	Player	Date	Opponent	Venue
8	Morne Steyn	1 Aug 2009	New Zealand	Durban
7	Percy Montgomery	17 Jun 2006	Scotland	Port Elizabeth
7	Percy Montgomery	24 Jun 2006	France	Cape Town

Pens	Player	Date	Opponent	Venue
7	Morné Steyn	8 Aug 2009	Australia	Cape Town
6	Gerald Bosch	28 Jun 1975	France	Pretoria
6	Joel Stransky	3 Aug 1996	Australia	Bloemfontein
6	Jannie de Beer	30 Oct 1999	Australia	Twickenham
6	Braam van Straaten	17 Jun 2000	England	Pretoria
6	Braam van Straaten	26 Aug 2000	Australia	Durban
6	Percy Montgomery	16 Jun 2001	France	Johannesburg
6	Louis Koen	14 Jun 2003	Scotland	Johannesburg
6	Morné Steyn	4 Sept 2010	Australia	Bloemfontein

Against:

Pens	Player	Date	For	Venue
8	Matt Burke	30 Oct 1999	Australia	Twickenham
8	Jonny Wilkinson	24 Jun 2000	England	Bloemfontein
7	Andrew Mehrtens	7 Aug 1999	New Zealand	Pretoria
7	Jonny Wilkinson	24 Nov 2001	England	Twickenham
7	Dan Carter	22 Jul 2006	New Zealand	Wellington

— MULTIPLE CONVERSIONS —

Percy Montgomery, who was the kicker in two of the Springboks' biggest victories, dominates the list of most conversions in a test match. He scored 12 conversions in the victory over Namibia in 2007 and nine against Wales in 1998. Stirling Mortlock scored five conversions for Australia in 2006 in their 49–0 win against South Africa in 2006.
For South Africa:

Conv	Player	Date	Opponent	Venue
12	Percy Montgomery	15 Aug 2007	Namibia	Cape Town
9	Percy Montgomery	27 Jun 1998	Wales	Pretoria
9	Butch James	9 Aug 2008	Argentina	Johannesburg
8	Percy Montgomery	6 Dec 1997	Scotland	Murrayfield

8	Gaffie du Toit	12 Jun 1999	Italy	Port Elizabeth
8	Gaffie du Toit	19 Jun 1999	Italy	Durban

Against:

Conv	Player	Date	For	Venue
5	Stirling Mortlock	15 Jul 2006	Australia	Brisbane
4	Paul McLean	27 Aug 1977	World XV	Pretoria
4	Angus Cameron	6 Aug 1955	British Isles	Johannesburg
4	Carlos Spencer	9 Aug 1997	New Zealand	Auckland
4	Andrew Mehrtens	19 Aug 2000	New Zealand	Johannesburg
4	Carlos Spencer	19 Jul 2003	New Zealand	Pretoria
4	Dan Carter	26 Aug 2006	New Zealand	Pretoria

— DROPPING IN —

Naas Botha, the Springboks' dropped goal king, kicked three dropped goals in a test match on two occasions, against South America in 1980 and against Ireland in 1981. In the 1999 Rugby World Cup, Jannie de Beer kicked five dropped goals in the victory over England in Paris. André Pretorius almost repeated this feat, also against England, when he kicked four dropped goals in 2006. No player has ever scored more than two dropped goals against South Africa in a test.
For South Africa:

DG	Player	Date	Opponent	Venue
5	Jannie de Beer	24 Oct 1999	England	Paris
4	André Pretorius	25 Nov 2006	England	Twickenham
3	Naas Botha	3 May 1980	South America	Durban
3	Naas Botha	6 Jun 1981	Ireland	Durban
3	Jaco van der Westhuyzen	27 Nov 2004	Scotland	Murrayfield

Against:

DG	Player	Date	Opponent	Venue
2	Guy Camberabero	29 July 1967	France	Johannesburg
2	Phil Bennett	13 July 1974	British Isles	Port Elizabeth
2	Jonny Wilkinson	18 Oct 2003	England	Perth

— MONOPOLY STEYN —

With his 25 points against Australia in 1996, Joel Stransky was the player who has single-handedly scored the most points in a test match for South Africa until Morné Steyn arrived on the scene. Steyn scored 31 points against New Zealand in a Tri-Nations game in Durban. His points consisted of one try, one conversion and eight penalties. Jonny Wilkinson seemingly beat South Africa on his own when he scored all England's points in their 27–22 victory over the Springboks in Bloemfontein in 2000, his tally consisting of 8 penalties and one dropped goal.

For South Africa:

Pts	Name	Opponents	Venue	Date
31	Morné Steyn	New Zealand	Durban	1 Aug 2009
25	Joel Stransky	Australia	Bloemfontein	3 Aug 1996
21	Jannie de Beer	Australia	Twickenham	30 Oct 1999
18	Braam van Straaten	England	Pretoria	17 Jun 2000
18	Braam van Straaten	Australia	Durban	26 Aug 2000
17	Braam van Straaten	England	Twickenham	2 Dec 2000
15	Okey Geffin	New Zealand	Cape Town	16 Jul 1949
15	André Joubert	England	Pretoria	4 Jun 1994
15	Joel Stransky	New Zealand	Johannesburg	24 Jun 1995
15	Braam van Straaten	New Zealand	Auckland	25 Aug 2001

Against:

Pts	Name	For	Venue	Date
27	Jonny Wilkinson	England	Bloemfontein	24 Jun 2000
21	Hugo Porta	South America	Bloemfontein	3 Apr 1992
18	Shane Howarth	New Zealand	Auckland	6 Aug 1994
17	Ronan O'Gara	Ireland	Dublin	13 Nov 2004
15	Thierry Lacroix	France	Durban	17 Jun 1995
15	Andrew Mehrtens	New Zealand	Christchurch	20 Jul 1996
15	Matthew Burke	Australia	Johannesburg	20 Aug 1998
15	Gerald Merceron	France	Durban	23 Jun 2001

— FREQUENT OPPONENTS —

The Australian scrumhalf George Gregan has the unique distinction of playing in 30 consecutive test matches against South Africa. His remarkable run against the Springboks began in the opening match of the 1995 Rugby World Cup in Cape Town, following which he started every game at number 9 until he retired at the end of the 2008 Tri-Nations.

His halfback partner in 23 of those tests was Stephen Larkham, who has played the second most tests against South Africa.

Apps	Name	Country	Career
30	George Gregan	Australia	1995–2007
23	Stephen Larkham	Australia	1998–2007
22	Justin Marshall	New Zealand	1996–2004
22	George Smith	Australia	2001–2009
21	Matt Giteau	Australia	2003–2010
21	Mils Muliaina	New Zealand	2003–2010
20	Nathan Sharpe	Australia	2002–2010

— CULLEN'S TEN —

Christian Cullen scored ten tries against South Africa in 15 test appearances for the All Blacks between 1996 and 2002, scoring two in a match on four occasions. Remarkably the prolific Jonah Lomu, who scored 37 tries in 63 caps for New Zealand, never managed to score a try in a dozen test matches against the Springboks.

Tries	Name	Country	Tests	Career
10	Christian Cullen	New Zealand	15	1996–2002
9	Joe Rokocoko	New Zealand	10	2003–07
7	Stirling Mortlock	Australia	17	2000–08
6	Matt Giteau	Australia	15	2003–08
6	Chris Latham	Australia	15	2000–06

— FREQUENT REFS —

Paddy O'Brien, who is currently the Referee Manager of the International Rugby Board, is the international referee who has handled the most of South Africa's test matches since Norman Sanson from Scotland became the first neutral referee in 1975.

Tests	Referee	Country	Won	Lost	Drawn	% Wins
12	Paddy O'Brien	New Zealand	7	5	–	58%
12	Alain Rolland	Ireland	7	5	–	58%
11	Stuart Dickinson	Australia	3	8	–	27%
10	Colin Hawke	New Zealand	7	3	–	70%
10	Steve Walsh	New Zealand	8	1	1	80%
9	Derek Bevan	Wales	7	2	–	78%
9	Ed Morrison	England	3	6	–	33%
8	Paul Honiss	New Zealand	3	5	–	38%
8	Peter Marshall	Australia	3	5	–	38%

— SOUTH AFRICAN REFEREES IN SA TESTS —

When Jonathan Kaplan officiated at the test match between South Africa and Namibia in 2007, he became just the fourth South African referee to be involved in a Springbok test match since neutral referees were introduced in 1977.

The complete list is:			
Johan Gouws	27 Aug 1977	South Africa 45, World XV 24	Pretoria
Steve Strydom	27 Mar 1982	South Africa 50, South America 18	Pretoria
Fransie Muller	3 Apr 1982	South Africa 12, South America 21	Bloemfontein
Jonathan Kaplan	15 Aug 2007	South Africa 105, Namibia 13	Cape Town

Note: Johann Meuwesen handled two test matches between South Africa and Western Samoa in 1995, and against Fiji in 1996, but he was from Namibia at the time.

— DECK OF CARDS —

The issuing of yellow and red coloured cards for disciplinary reasons was introduced in 1995. Technically the first Springbok to receive a yellow card was Percy Montgomery, from Australian referee Peter Marshall in the 48th minute against New Zealand at Ellis Park on 19 July 1997, although in those days a yellow card meant a formal caution and not a ten-minute spell in the sin bin. Subsequently eleven other South African players received 'yellow card cautions' until this was changed to sinbinnings in 2000. They were issued to James Small, Joost van der Westhuizen (2), Krynauw Otto, Mark Andrews, Henry Honiball, Adrian Garvey, Robbie Kempson (2), Corné Krige and Johan Erasmus.

The first Springbok to be sinbinned was Robbie Fleck between the 64th and 74th minutes by Irish referee Alan Lewis against Canada at East London on 16 June 2000.

To date 70 yellow card sinbinnings have been handed out to 43 different Springboks by 25 different referees. One of these, Faan Rautenbach against Australia at Brisbane in July 2002, was awarded retrospectively after the independent citing commissioner found him guilty of punching. The figure also ignores the second 'yellow' Percy Montgomery received, turning it into a red, against Wales in Cardiff in November 2005.

— THE SPRINGBOK EMBLEM 1906–2009 —

1906–1933

1937–1962

1963–1964

1965–1989

1996–2003

1992–1995

2004–current

— SPRINGBOK JERSEYS SINCE 1992 —

1992

1995 Rugby World Cup

2002 against France

2000

1997

1999 Rugby World Cup

2003 Rugby World Cup

2004

2006

2007 Rugby World Cup

2011 Rugby World Cup

All jerseys until 2007 by courtesy of Derek Roos, from his private collection. The 2011 jersey by courtesy of SA Rugby.

The most yellow cards have been awarded against Schalk Burger (6), Victor Matfield (4), Robbie Kempson, De Wet Barry, Breyton Paulse and Bakkies Botha (3).

Due to sinbinnings, South Africa have been forced to play with only 13 players for some time in four test matches; against Australia in August 2004, Scotland in November 2004, Australia in July 2005 and Tonga in September 2007.

Referee Steve Walsh has handed out the most yellow cards to South African players (8), followed by Paddy O'Brien (6), Chris White and Stuart Dickinson (5), Alain Rolland, Joel Jutge, Paul Honiss and Steve Lander (4).

Only 27 yellow cards have been received by Springbok opponents. This includes the first, which was awarded in error in the 70th minute to Australian centre James Holbeck at Pretoria on 23 August 1997 when referee Paddy O'Brien got confused: sinbinnings were not in use in test matches at the time, but were used in Super 12 games!

— FAST YELLOWS —

The quickest yellow card from the start of a match is when Schalk Burger received one from referee Christophe Berdos after 32 seconds against the British and Irish Lions in Pretoria on 27 June 2009.

Jaque Fourie was sinbinned within seconds of coming on as a replacement against Wales in Cardiff on 8 November 2008, while other fast cards as a substitute were handed to Schalk Burger (3 mins) against Australia at Johannesburg on 23 July 2005, Pedrie Wannenberg (2 mins) against New Zealand at Durban on 23 June 2007 and Bismarck du Plessis (2 mins) against Wales in Cardiff on 24 November 2007.

— SEEING RED —

The following Springboks have been shown red cards during matches:

Name	Date	Opponents (Venue)	Min	Referee
James Small	14 Aug 1993	Australia (Brisbane)	30th	Ed Morrison
Keith Andrews	2 Nov 1993	Tucumán (Tucumán)	65th	Efraim Sklar

Name	Date	Opponents (Venue)	Min	Referee
Hannes Strydom	2 Nov 1993	Tucumán (Tucumán)	65th	Efraim Sklar
Adri Geldenhuys	19 Jul 1994	Manawatu (Palmerston North)	70th	Steve Walsh
James Dalton	3 Jun 1995	Canada (Port Elizabeth)	70th	David McHugh
André Venter	9 Aug 1997	New Zealand (Auckland)	47th	Derek Bevan
Toks van der Linde	11 Nov 1997	French Barbarians (Biarritz)	39th	Joel Dume
Brendan Venter	15 Oct 1999	Uruguay (Glasgow)	40th	Peter Marshall
Marius Joubert	17 Aug 2002	Australia (Johannesburg)	70th	Paddy O'Brien
Jannes Labuschagne	23 Nov 2002	England (Twickenham)	22nd	Paddy O'Brien
Percy Montgomery	19 Nov 2005	Wales (Cardiff)	71st	Stuart Dickinson

Against:

Name	Date	For (Venue)	Min	Referee
Gareth Rees	3 Jun 1995	Canada (Port Elizabeth)	70th	David McHugh
Rod Snow	3 Jun 1995	Canada (Port Elizabeth)	70th	David McHugh
Garin Jenkins	2 Sep 1995	Wales (Johannesburg)	75th	Joel Dume

— IT'S A NUMBERS GAME —

Photographic evidence shows that the Springboks wore numbers on the back of their green shirts for the first time in 1906 on the Springbok tour to the United Kingdom. For many years the numbering did not follow today's numbering sequence. Up until 1951 the fullback wore '1', with the rest of the backs following on up to '7'; the pack wore numbers 8–15, with the eightman as '15'. For the series against Australia in 1953 and against the British Lions in 1955, the numbering changed, with the fullback wearing '15', almost the same as these days, with the exception that the left wing wore '13' and the centres wore '11' and '12'. In 1956, on the tour to Australia and New Zealand, they went back to the sequence of '1' for the fullback. In 1960 they reverted to the fullback as '15'. Up until 1976 the left wing wore 13, but it was changed to '11' in 1977, with the centres wearing '12' and '13'. In 1968, when four substitutes were allowed for the first time, the subs wore '16' to '19', but that was no guide to their positions. From 1972 the Springboks were allowed six subs on the bench. In the 1990s guidelines came into force and the substitutes were originally numbered from the back, with the backs wearing '16' to '18' and the forwards '19' to '21'. In 1998 the numbers of subs was increased to seven and in 2000 the numbering of replacements changed to today's convention of '16' to '19' as the forward subs ('16' as the reserve hooker, '17' as the reserve prop, '18' as the reserve lock and '19' as the reserve loose-forward), and '20' to '22' for the backs ('20' as the reserve scrumhalf, '21' as the reserve flyhalf/centre and '22' as the reserve wing/fullback).

The first players to sit on the bench for the Springboks were: Tiny Neethling, Don Walton, HO de Villiers and Piet Uys, who warmed the bench against the British Lions in 1968.

Before 1937 the numbers on the jerseys were in black on a white background. From 1937 the background changed to old gold. From 1958 no background was used, only the old gold number on the green jersey.

Teams in South Africa were numbered and announced as follows:

1949 to 1954		1955 to 1976	
1	Fullback	15	Fullback
2	Left wing	13	Left wing
4	Centre	11	Centre
5	Centre	12	Centre
3	Right wing	14	Right wing
6	Flyhalf	10	Flyhalf
7	Scrumhalf	9	Scrumhalf
8	Loosehead prop	1	Loosehead prop
9	Hooker	2	Hooker

	1949 to 1954		1955 to 1976
10	Tighthead prop	3	Tighthead prop
11	Flank	6	Flank
12	Lock	4	Lock
13	Lock	5	Lock
14	Flank	7	Flank
15	Eightman	8	Eightman
	1977 to 1994		**1995 to date**
15	Fullback	15	Fullback
11	Left wing	14	Right wing
12	Centre	13	Outside Centre
13	Centre	·14	Inside Centre
14	Right wing	11	Left wing
10	Flyhalf	10	Flyhalf
9	Scrumhalf	9	Scrumhalf
1	Loosehead prop	8	Eightman
2	Hooker	7	Blindside flank
3	Tighthead prop	6	Openside flank
6	Flank	5	Lock
4	Lock	4	Lock
5	Lock	3	Tighthead prop
7	Flank	2	Hooker
8	Eightman	1	Loosehead prop

— PLAYED IN ALL POSITIONS IN THE BACKS —

Brent Russell gained 23 Springboks test caps, of which only seven were starts. His debut was as a replacement flyhalf against Wales at Bloemfontein in 2002, coming on in the 47th minute for Ricardo Loubscher. The original number ten, André Pretorius, switched to fullback. Brent went on to make a further three appearances at flyhalf, seven at fullback, nine on the wing, and two at centre, before rounding off his full set on his 16th appearance by coming on as a replacement scrumhalf for the last 14 minutes for Jaco van der Westhuizen against Wales in Cardiff in November 2004.

The only other player to have appeared in all possible positions amongst the backs is **Ruan Pienaar**. Ruan has made 30 test appearances, his debut coming as a replacement fullback for Percy Montgomery against New Zealand at Pretoria in August 2006. He then made 14 appearances at scrumhalf, 2 in the centre, and 8 at flyhalf. Pienaar completed his set with an appearance as a replacement wing for JP Pietersen during the RWC semi-final encounter with Argentina in Paris in 2007.

— STARTED IN FOUR OR MORE DIFFERENT POSITIONS —

Danie Craven was capped once at eightman, twice at flyhalf, once at centre and 12 times at scrumhalf. He also played fullback on tour in 1937 against Queensland.

Boy Louw played six tests at loosehead prop, seven at tighthead prop, two at lock, two at flank and one at eightman. He also played hooker in four tour matches.

In modern times it's François Steyn who has shown his versatility, making three starts at fullback, one on the left wing, eight at centre (seven inside and one outside), and one at flyhalf – and all that by the time he was 21!

— FORWARD AND BACK —

Gerrie Sonnekus made his South Africa debut at scrumhalf against the British Isles in the third test in Port Elizabeth in 1974. Ten years later, in 1984, he gained his 2nd and 3rd caps as eightman against England.

Danie Craven played one test as eightman against Australia at the Sydney Cricket Ground for his tenth cap. His other 15 tests were all as a back (12 as scrumhalf, two at flyhalf and one at centre).

Pierre Spies came on as a substitute wing in the last 16 minutes against the British and Irish Lions at Coca-Cola Park in Johannesburg on 4 July 2009 to add to his tally of 21 caps as a backrow.

Three Northern Transvaal (now: Blue Bulls) wings ended up playing as flanks for the Springboks: **Louis ('Ouboet') Strydom, Daan Retief** and **Pierre Spies.**

— THREE POSITIONS IN ONE SERIES —

Versatile Manie Geere only won five caps, all in successive games during the five-test series against Australia in 1933. He began at Cape Town and Durban as lock, switched to flank for the third test in Johannesburg, before playing prop in the final two tests at Port Elizabeth and Bloemfontein.

— APPEARED IN THE FRONT-ROW AND BACK-ROW —

Seven players have experienced some game time for the Springboks in both the front and back row: Boy Louw and Manie Geere did so, along with prop Fanie Louw who gained 11 caps in his favoured position but also started at flank against the Wallabies at Durban in 1933.

The list is completed with four modern-day contemporaries, all of them hookers who were pressed into service as replacement flanks: Naka Drotské, Chris Rossouw, Hanyani Shimange and Chiliboy Ralepelle.

— MOST CAPPED BY POSITION —

(Including replacement appearances)		
Prop:	80	Os du Randt
Hooker:	87	John Smit (plus 15 at prop)
Lock:	105	Victor Matfield
Flank:	61	Schalk Burger (plus 2 at No. 8)
Eightman:	42	Gary Teichmann
Scrumhalf:	87	Joost van der Westhuizen (plus 2 on the wing)
Flyhalf:	37	Butch James (plus 3 at centre)
Centre:	53	Jean de Villiers (plus 14 on the wing)
Wing:	67	Bryan Habana (plus 1 at centre)
Fullback:	87	Percy Montgomery (plus 5 at flyhalf, 1 on the wing and 9 at centre)
Replacement:	43	Ollie le Roux

— MONSIEUR LE DROP —

Naas Botha has kicked the most dropped goals for South Africa, with a record 18 in just 28 test appearances between 1980 and 1992. Naas twice landed three dropped goals in a single test, against South America at Durban on 3 May 1980, and against Ireland at Durban on 6 June 1981. He also kicked dropped goals on his test debut and his last three appearances.

Hansie Brewis kicked dropped goals in four consecutive tests, a South African record, namely the last test against New Zealand in 1949 and the first three tests on the Springbok tour to the United Kingdom and France in 1952–53 against Scotland, Ireland and Wales.

— SPRINGBOK LEGENDS: FRIK DU PREEZ —

FRIK DU PREEZ FACTFILE
Born: 28 November 1935 in the Rustenburg district, North West Province
Province: Northern Transvaal
Caps: 38 (W24, D6, L8)
Scoring: 1 try, 1 conversion, 2 penalties – 11 points
Springbok debut: vs England on 7 January 1961 (Twickenham, London)

Frik du Preez sets off on one of his storming runs.

Frik du Preez first gained Springbok colours as a member of Avril Malan's 1960–61 team to the UK and France, when he was selected as a flank forward. It was in this position that he played his first test match, against England at Twickenham on 7 January 1961. In his career, which spanned from 1960 to 1971, he played in 38 test matches, a South African record that was equalled by Jan Ellis in 1976 and stood for many years until James Small surpassed the mark on 19 July 1997 against New Zealand at Ellis Park. The well-built Du Preez was a hero in South African rugby, especially for his ability to run and kick like a backline player. Dr Danie Craven wrote the following about him: 'Frik du Preez is a once-in-a-lifetime phenomenon. I don't think Frik himself ever realised how much he was capable of. He was a forward and a back rolled into one.' Amazingly, he only scored one test try, against the British Lions in 1968 on his beloved Loftus Versfeld in Pretoria. What a gem of a try it was. He received the ball from his great friend Mof Myburgh after Tiny Naudé won it in a line-out, and ran forty metres, bouncing off several Lions players on his way, to score in the corner. In all Springbok matches Du Preez scored 87 points in 87 games. These points were made up from 12 tries, 15 conversions and 7 penalty goals. In 2000 he received the biggest award in South African rugby when he was chosen as the Springbok Rugby Player of the Century.

— FIRST REPLACEMENTS —

South Africa first used a replacement in an international on 2 August 1969, when Northern Transvaal's scrumhalf Piet Uys came on for captain Dawie de Villiers, who had dislocated a shoulder, against Australia at Ellis Park, Johannesburg. The previous year the IRB had ruled that replacements could be used in tests, but only after an independent doctor had decreed that the substituted player was unfit to continue.

Temporary replacements to cover for players who had been cut on the field of play were first introduced in 1993. South Africa's first such 'blood bin' replacement was James Small, who came on for Gavin Johnson between the 32nd and 37th minutes against New Zealand at Eden Park on 6 August 1994.

Tactical substitutions were made legal for the first time by the IRB on 4 November 1996. South Africa used two tactical subs against Argentina on 9 November at the Ferrocarril Oeste Stadium in Buenos Aires in a 46–15 victory, the first seeing Toks van der Linde, the Western Province prop, coming on for Dawie Theron in the 62nd minute. South Africa first used all six substitutes then allowed against the British and Irish Lions in the third test at Ellis Park on 5 July 1997 when Henry Honiball (for Percy Montgomery), Justin Swart (Jannie de Beer), Werner Swanepoel (Joost van der Westhuizen), Fritz van Heerden (Gary Teichmann), Adrian Garvey (Os du Randt) and Naka Drotské (James Dalton) took to the field.

From the beginning of 1998 the IRB allowed seven substitutes on the bench. In the Springboks' third test of that year, against Wales at Loftus Versfeld on 27 June 1998, the Springboks first used all seven players on the bench; McNeil Hendricks (Stefan Terblanche), Henry Honiball (Pieter Muller), Werner Swanepoel (Joost van der Westhuizen), Andrew Aitken (Gary Teichmann), Bob Skinstad (Mark Andrews), Ollie le Roux (Adrian Garvey) and Naka Drotské (James Dalton).

— JEWISH LUCK —

There is a saying in South Africa: 'With a Jewish player in the side, the Springboks can't lose!!' The ten Jews who have so far played for South Africa are: Maurice Zimerman (1931), Fred Smollan (1933), Louis Babrow (1937), Cecil Moss (1949), Okey Geffin (1949), Wilf Rosenberg (1955), Joe Kaminer (1958), Syd Nomis (1965), Alan Menter (1968) and Joel Stransky (1993).

In all, Jewish players have played in 78 tests for the Springboks, being on the winning side an incredible 57 (73%), drawing six and losing 15 (19%). Syd Nomis is the most capped Jewish player, with 25 consecutive tests between 1967 and 1972. This was a South African record for many years until it was broken by Gary Teichmann in 1997.

Louis Babrow was chosen for the third and final test against New Zealand in 1937. This test fell on the Jewish Day of Atonement, but Babrow decided to play, arguing that, with the time difference, he would have played the game before the Day of Atonement had dawned in South Africa. Okey Geffin's family were refugees from Russia. Their name was originally Galombik. When his father arrived by ship in Cape Town from Poneves in Russia, he was faced by a wanted sign for a horse thief called Galombik, so he used his second name, Gavin, as his surname. However, his pronunciation flummoxed the officials, who registered him as Geffin.

Wilf Rosenberg, a medical doctor by profession, was the most controversial of our Jewish Springboks. Rosenberg decided to play rugby league in the United Kingdom, a heresy that caused severe ructions in those amateur days. The most influential Jewish Springbok of all time is certainly Joel Stransky. He booted himself into history with that famous dropped goal in extra time in the 1995 World Cup final at Ellis Park in Johannesburg which won the World Cup for the Springboks.

— IRB INTERNATIONAL PLAYER OF THE YEAR —

The IRB International Player of the Year is an accolade awarded annually by the International Rugby Board. It is awarded to the player who is adjudged to have been the best performer In rugby Internationals in the prececeding season. This award was first made In 2001. Schalk Burger (in 2004) and Bryan Habana (in 2007) are the only Springboks to have received this award so far. Other Springboks who were also nominated are: Joe van Niekerk (2002), Marius Joubert (2004), Bryan

Habana (2005), Victor Matfield (2005 & 2010), Fourie du Preez (2006 & 2009) and François Steyn (2009). The complete list of winners is:

Year	Player	Country
2001	Keith Wood	Ireland
2002	Fabian Galthie	France
2003	Jonny Wilkinson	England
2004	Schalk Burger	South Africa
2005	Daniel Carter	New Zealand
2006	Richie McCaw	New Zealand
2007	Bryan Habana	South Africa
2008	Shane Williams	Wales
2009	Richie McCaw	New Zealand
2010	Richie Mccaw	New Zealand

— MEMBERS OF PARLIAMENT —

The following Springboks have become Members of Parliament:

Jack Hirsch

Bob Loubser

Paul Roos

'Boy' de Villiers

Willem Delport

Herman van Broekhuizen (also Minister Plenipotentiary to Holland at the outbreak of the Second World War)

Frank Waring (also Minister of Sport)

Dawie de Villiers (also Minister of Industry, Trade and Tourism as well as South African Ambassador to Great Britain)

— SPRINGBOKS WHO PLAYED AGAIN AFTER RETIREMENT —

George Daneel, who died in 2004 at the age of 100 (the only Springbok so far to reach this milestone), played for Western Province from 1925 to 1929. In 1929 he quit rugby to go into church work. By 1931 he was coaching Pretoria University and playing for them when he received a telegram from 'Oubaas' Markötter inviting him to the Springbok trials. He went to the first trials but missed the final trials because he had to attend his ordainment as minister at Calvinia. Daneel was selected for the 1931–32 tour to the United Kingdom, where he played in all four tests. After this tour he retired from all rugby at the age of 28. In 1940 he was an Army Chaplain at Potchefstroom during the Second World War. Western Transvaal asked him to help out when their captain Nic Bierman, also a Springbok during the 1931–32 tour to the UK, sustained an injury. Daneel agreed and played his last provincial game at the age of 36.

Gerry Brand played his last provincial rugby for Western Province on 25 June 1938 against the British Isles and his last test match in the first test against the British Isles on 6 August 1938 at Ellis Park. 'He was injured on the Thursday before the next test and could not play in the final two internationals,' Dr Craven writes in his book *Springbok Story 1949–1953*. 'Gerry Brand had staged a comeback, mainly to help the combined Hamiltons–Villagers team, and at a ripe old rugby age was once again selected to play for Western Province in their annual match against Transvaal.' This game took place on 7 July 1945, which means that he played at the age of 38 years and 270 days, very unusual for a backline player.

Mannetjies Roux retired after the 1970 season in which he played in all four tests against New Zealand. His final game was the Currie Cup final in which his team, Griquas, beat Northern Transvaal by 11–9 against all odds. In 1975 he coached the North Eastern Cape team which played against the French touring side at Aliwal North. In the second half of the game, centre Droes van Vuuren left the field with an injury and was replaced by Roux, who showed some class with a few good tackles.

Piet Visagie broke his leg early in the 1972 season when playing for Griqualand West against South West Africa in Windhoek. He had been certain to play for South Africa in the one-off test against England later that year, but he decided to retire from the game. In 1974, by which time he coached Griquas, Piet Bothma, the Griquas flyhalf, was injured during a game against Transvaal at Ellis Park and Visagie ran on as replacement for his last game in the Griqua jersey.

Lofty Nel retired from first-class rugby at the end of the 1973 season in which he played for South Eastern Transvaal, having played his last test against the All Blacks in 1970. In 1974 he was appointed as team manager for South Eastern Transvaal when they went to play a game against Eastern Province in Port Elizabeth. Polla Fourie, who was to make his Springbok debut later in the year against the British Lions, withdrew just before the game, and Nel took his place. He was already 38 years of age and made a further comeback after this game, playing his last game for SE Transvaal in 1974 at the age of 39. Coincidently there was another Springbok of 1970 in the SE Transvaal team, namely Johan Spies, who also retired at the end of 1973 to take up farming in the Middelburg area. He was persuaded to play again, and the little-known team fielded three Springboks in 1974.

HO de Villiers played his last game for Western Province in 1969. After the Springbok tour to the United Kingdom in 1969–70, he had several knee operations. In 1975 he played one last game for Western Province against North Eastern Cape when Dawie Snyman was not available.

Eben Jansen, the brother of Springbok Joggie, played his provincial rugby for Free State and Boland. At the end of 1987 he retired from the game and went into coaching; he coached the Boland provincial side for many years. In 1994 he was chosen as assistant coach of the Central Unions touring team to Ireland. Because of injury he went on as a replacement against the Irish Colleges.

Louis Koen, who played his last test for South Africa in 2003, was the Boland Rugby Union's kicking coach in 2010. Injuries in the team compelled him to made a comeback for Boland against the Falcons at the age of 35, scoring 12 points in the match via three conversions and two penalties.

— FULL HOUSES —

Only three Springboks have scored in every way possible (try, conversion, penalty goal and dropped goal) in a single test.

Joel Stransky did so against Australia at Newlands on 25 May 1995 in the opening match of the 1995 Rugby World Cup during a 27–18 victory.

André Pretorius became the second player to achieve the feat against New Zealand at Durban on 18 August 2002, while Derick Hougaard became the most recent, against Samoa in Brisbane on 1 November 2003 at the Rugby World Cup in a 60–10 win.

For South Africa:

Name	Opponent (Venue)	Date	T	C	P	D	Pts
Joel Stransky	Australia (Cape Town)	25 May 1995	1	1	4	1	22

Name	Opponent (Venue)	Date	T	C	P	D	Pts
André Pretorius	New Zealand (Durban)	10 Aug 2002	1	2	2	1	18
Derick Hougaard	Samoa (Brisbane)	1 Nov 2003	1	5	1	1	21

Against:

Name	For (Venue)	Date	T	C	P	D	Pts
Hugo Porta	S America (Bloemfontein)	3 Apr 1982	1	1	4	1	21*
Rob Andrew	England (Pretoria)	4 Jun 1994	1	2	5	1	27
Diego Dominguez	Italy (Genoa)	17 Nov 2001	1	1	3	1	19
Charlie Hodgson	England (Twickenham)	20 Nov 2004	1	2	5	1	27

* Porta was captain of the South American team

— SAME SURNAME IN SAME POSITION —

In the third test match against the British Isles on 3 September 1910 at Newlands, the two props were Dougie and Boy Morkel.

In the one-off test match against Ireland on 13 May 1961 at Newlands, Cape Town, the two wings were Hennie and Ben-Piet van Zyl.

In the test match against Ireland on 10 January 1970, the two centres were Mannetjies and Tonie Roux.

— MOST PLAYERS WITH THE SAME SURNAME —

In the test against Ireland on 13 May 1961 at Newlands, Cape Town, there were four Van Zyls in the team, namely Hennie and Ben-Piet on the wing, Hugo on the flank and Piet at lock. They were not related.

In the second test against South America on 3 May 1980 at King's Park in Durban, there were four Du Plessis' in the team. Willie (centre), Tommy (scrum-half), Daan (prop) and Morné (eigthman). They were also not related.

— THE DU PLESSIS ELEVEN —

When Jannie du Plessis made his Springbok debut against Australia in a Tri-Nations game at the Telstra Stadium in Sydney on 7 July 2007, he became the eleventh Du Plessis to play for South Africa. The previous record was held by the famous Morkel family from Somerset West, of which ten played for South Africa between 1903 and 1928.

The eleven Du Plessis' who played for South Africa:

Initials	Name	Caps	Year
BW	Bismarck	36	2007–10
CJ	Carel	12	1982–89
DC	Daan	2	1977–80
F	Felix	3	1949
JN	Jannie	24	2007–10
M	Morné	22	1971–80
MJ	Michael	8	1984–89
NJ	Nic	5	1921–24
PG	Piet	1	1972
TD	Tommy	2	1980
W	Willie	14	1980–82

Carel, Michael and Willie were brothers.
Felix was the father of Morné.

— THE MORKEL DYNASTY —

The ten Morkels who played for South Africa:

Initials	Name	Caps	Year
DFT	Dougie	9	1906–13
DJA	Andrew	1	1903
HJL	Harry	1	1921
HW	Henry	2	1921
JA	Royal	2	1921
JWH	Jackie	5	1912–13

Initials	Name	Caps	Year
PG	Gerhard	8	1912–21
PK	PK	1	1928
WH	Boy	9	1910–21
WS	Sommie	4	1906

Dougie and Sommie were brothers.
Gerhard and Jackie were brothers.
Harry and Royal were brothers.
Boy was a cousin of Gerhard and Jackie.
Gerhard and Jackie were cousins of Dougie and Sommie

— KEEPING UP WITH THE JONESES —

When the Springboks beat Wales 38–36 on 6 November 2004 at the Millennium Stadium in Cardiff, there were six players named Jones in the Wales starting line-up. The Wales team that day was: Gareth Thomas (capt), Hal Luscombe, Sonny Parker, Gavin Henson, Shane Williams, **Stephen Jones**, Dwayne Peel, **Duncan Jones**, **Steve Jones**, **Adam Jones**, Brent Cockbain, Michael Owen, **Dafydd Jones**, Colin Charvis and **Ryan Jones**.

When the Springboks beat Wales 20–15 on 8 November 2008 at the Millennium Stadium in Cardiff, there were six players named Jones in the squad of 22. Adam Jones (prop), Alun-Wyn Jones (lock), Ryan Jones (flank) and Stephen Jones (flyhalf) in the starting line-up and Duncan Jones and Dafydd Jones on the bench. The replacement Jones boys didn't go on.

— PLAYED IN THREE SEPARATE DECADES —

Chris Koch, the Boland prop, made his debut for the Springboks on 13 August 1949 against the All Blacks at Johannesburg aged 21. His international career ended with a 22nd cap on 23 July 1960, again against the All Blacks in Cape Town, thus achieving the remarkable feat of having played test match rugby in the 1940s, 1950s and 1960s.

— CAPTAIN ON DEBUT —

In the history of South African rugby twelve Springbok captains were also making their debut. Of these, five played in their only test and Basie Vivier was already a Springbok (1951), but never played in a test match before 1956. Corné Krige has the distinction of captaining, on debut, a Springbok team which scored over a century of points in their victory of 101-0 against Italy in 1999.

Name	Opponents	Date	Result
HH Castens*	Great Britain	30 Jul 1891	Lost 0–4
Bob Snedden*	Great Britain	29 Aug 1891	Lost 0–3
Ferdy Aston	Great Britain	30 Jul 1896	Lost 0–8
Alex Frew*	Great Britain	29 Aug 1903	Drew 10–10
PK Albertyn	Great Britain	16 Aug 1924	Won 7–3
Felix du Plessis	New Zealand	16 Jul 1949	Won 15–11
Basil Kenyon*	New Zealand	17 Sep 1949	Won 11–8
Basie Vivier	Australia	26 May 1956	Won 9–0
Des van Jaarsveldt*	Scotland	30 Apr 1960	Won 18–10
Wynand Claassen	Ireland	30 May 1981	Won 23–15
François Pienaar	France	26 Jun 1993	Drew 20–20
Corné Krige	Italy	19 Jun 1999	Won 101–0

* Only test appearance.

Frew had already gained three caps for Scotland, but none as skipper.

The following five players went on to captain South Africa in every one of their test appearances: Pienaar (29 tests), Claassen (7), Vivier (5), Albertyn (4) and Du Plessis (3).

— IN THE RIGHT PLACE AT THE RIGHT TIME —

In 1903, just before the final test at Newlands, the three Springbok selectors, Barry Heatlie, Percy Jones and Biddy Anderson, were discussing the team in the Café Royal in Church Street, Cape Town, wondering where they would find big forwards, when John Botha walked in, on holiday from the Transvaal. He played lock in that third test.

Incidentally, another John (Bakkies) Botha has played lock for South Africa, making his debut in 2002.

— SELECTORIAL BLUNDER —

In 1906 the Springbok selectors confused the two Marsbergs who were playing for Griquas: Artie, a wing, and Archie, a fullback, and chose Artie as fullback for the tour to the British Isles instead of his brother Archie. The selectors only realised their mistake on the *Gascon*, the ship that carried the team to the United Kingdom. Artie Marsberg turned out to be one of the finds of the tour and played in three tests. In 1910, when Great Britain visited South Africa, the selectors rectified their mistake by choosing Archie for the first test even though he was at the end of his career.

Bert and Jock Kipling were another set of brothers playing for Griquas. Jock was a good forward and an occasional hooker, and Bert was a hooker. The selectors intended selecting Jock but chose Bert instead for the tour to the British Isles in 1931–32. He played for South Africa until 1933.

— WELL-TRAVELLED BERGH —

Ferdie Bergh represented four different provinces in four consecutive test match series.

In 1931 he played for South Western Districts; in 1933 for Griqualand West; 1937 for Transvaal; and in 1938 for Northern Transvaal. He made his first-class debut for Western Transvaal in 1928. Bergh was a student at the University of Stellenbosch (Maties) in 1928 and 1929. Interestingly he never actually played for Western Province.

— WP DOMINATION —

Eleven players from Western Province have simultaneously appeared in a Springbok starting line-up on five occasions – the most from a single province.

The five occasions were:

v Great Britain (third test), 5 September 1891 at Newlands, Cape Town.
v Great Britain (third test), 12 September 1903 at Newlands, Cape Town.
v New Zealand (third test), 18 August 1928 at Crusader Ground, Port Elizabeth.

v New Zealand (fourth test), 1 September 1928 at Newlands, Cape Town.
v England (second test), 24 June 2000 at Free State Stadium, Bloemfontein.

— CAPPED FROM ABROAD —

The South African Rugby Union were always very strict about South African players playing overseas, considering them ineligible for selection. In the last few years, however, it has been accepted that rugby is now a global game, and since 2003 players playing overseas have been selected for South Africa. Rudolf Straueli was instrumental in bringing Thinus Delport back to South Africa prior to the 2003 Rugby World Cup. When Jake White became coach in 2004, he realised that he would not win the RWC in 2007 without the overseas players. He convinced Percy Montgomery to return to South Africa, a decision that played a big role in the Springboks' success. The South African Rugby Union decided in 2008 that the Springbok selectors are allowed to choose two players that are playing overseas.

The full list of players capped while playing overseas is:

Name	Club, Country (Caps, Years)
Jaco van der Westhuyzen	Leicester Tigers, England (8 caps, 2004)
	NEC Green Rockets, Japan (6 caps, 2005-06)
Percy Montgomery	Newport Gwent Dragons, Wales (11 caps, 2004)
	Perpignan, France (2 caps, 2008)
Breyton Paulse	Clermont Auvergne, France (1 cap, 2005)
André Snyman	Leeds Tykes, England (2 caps, 2006)
Danie Coetzee	London Irish, England (1 cap, 2006)
John Smit	Clermont Auvergne, France (3 caps, 2007-08)
Butch James	Bath, England (14 caps, 2008-2010)
CJ van der Linde	Leinster, Ireland (2 caps, 2009)
Jean de Villiers	Munster, Ireland (1 cap, 2009)
BJ Botha	Ulster, Ireland (8 caps, 2009-10)

Name	Club, Country (Caps, Years)
François Steyn	Racing Metro, France (6 caps, 2010)
Joe van Niekerk	Toulon, France (1 cap,
Ruan Pienaar	Munster, Ireland (4 caps, 2010)

— WESTERN TRANSVAAL SPRINGBOKS? —

WH 'Boy' Morkel played for Transvaal in 1920 and at the end of that year he was nominated by Transvaal for the trials to be held in April 1921 for the first tour to Australia and New Zealand. Early in 1921 he started farming in the district of Boskop near Potchefstroom and in March 1921 was elected as a member of the Potchefstroom Town Council during their annual general meeting. In 1921 Morkel did not play for Western Transvaal, and neither did he play for Transvaal. He went to the trials and was chosen as the vice-captain of the tour, the captain being Theo Pienaar. Pienaar couldn't make the side for the two tests in Australia and the three tests against New Zealand, and Morkel lead the team. Morkel, one of 10 Morkels to play for South Africa, made his first-class debut for Western Province in 1908 and played for them until 1914. In 1920 he started playing for Transvaal. He played his last game for Transvaal in 1924. In 1925 he started playing for Western Transvaal and in 1927, at the age of 42, he played his last provincial game.

Basie Vivier, who played for Free State in 1955, was nominated for the 1956 trials by the same province at the end of the 1955 season. Early in 1956 Vivier moved to Stilfontein in Western Transvaal. He attended the trials before playing for Western Transvaal and was chosen as captain of the Springbok tour to Australia and New Zealand. He never played for Western Transvaal because he retired from rugby after the 1956 tour. The Free State Rugby Union still acknowledges him as a Free State Springbok captain. The following article appeared in the Western Chronicle and Potchefstroom Budget on Friday, 20 April, 1956: 'RUGBY BOARD CONGRATULATES W.T.R.U. Official notification has been received by the Western Transvaal Rugby Union from the South African Board that the following players of the W.T.R.U. have been selected for the tour of Australia and New Zealand namely, SS Vivier (Captain), HN Walker and JT Claassen.'

The Western Transvaal Rugby Union claims that both Morkel and Vivier are Western Transvaal Springboks on the grounds that both lived in their area when they became Springbok captains. This matter will still be debated for a very long time.

— CLUB REPRESENTATION —

Eight members of the 1921 Springbok team to Australia and New Zealand were all playing for the same club at the time of selection, viz. Somerset West. They were JS Weepner, PG Morkel, WH Morkel, HW Morkel, JA Morkel, HJL Morkel, PJ Mostert and H Scholtz.

— LONG TIME, NO KICKS —

South Africa played against Scotland, Wales and England for the first time on the 1906 tour to the UK. It took these countries 54 years, 58 years and 63 years respectively to kick their first goal of any kind in a test match against South Africa. The players who achieved these feats were Arthur Smith (conversion for Scotland at Port Elizabeth in 1960); Keith Bradshaw (penalty for Wales at Durban in 1964); and Bob Hiller (penalty for England at Twickenham in 1969).

— FIRST GAME AND OUT —

Andrew Morkel was injured in the first game on the 1906–07 tour to the British Isles and never played again on tour.

Jack Siedle was injured in the first game of the 1921 tour to Australia and New Zealand and never played again on tour.

Jock van Niekerk was injured in the first match of the 1931–32 tour to the British Isles and never played again on tour.

Thomas Holliday, centre of Ronald Cove-Smith's British and Ireland's side in 1924, was hurt in the opening match and never played again on tour.

Stuart Lane, the British and Irish Lions flank in 1980, was injured in the first minute of the first game against Eastern Province and never again played on tour.

— NEVER PLAYED ON TOUR —

Wilfrid Gaisford, fullback of Ronald Cove-Smith's British and Ireland side in 1924, was hurt in the first training session the team had and did not play in any match.

During 1956 on the tour to Australia and New Zealand, **Basie van Wyk** broke his leg before he had played a match and did not play at all on the tour.

Louis Casaux, the French forward of Michel Celaya's 1958 side in South Africa, was hurt in training before the opening match and did not play on tour.

Kerneels Cronjé got hurt in an unofficial match in Australia in 1965 and never again played on tour.

— LIKED SOUTH AFRICA —

GM Cooke, a member of the Australian touring side in 1933, came back to South Africa and played for Transvaal in 1936 and 1937 before returning to Australia and playing for the Wallabies again.

Grahame Thorne, the 1970 All Black centre, returned to South Africa after the 1970 tour and married a South African woman he had met on tour. He played for Northern Transvaal and Natal and if the Springboks' tour to New Zealand in 1973 had not been called off, he would have represented the Springboks against his country of birth. His son Bruce played for the Golden Lions from 1996 to 2000.

John Robbie joined the British and Irish Lions team in 1980 as a replacement scrumhalf. He returned to South Africa and nearly gained his Springbok colours when he sat on the bench for South Africa in 1984.

— CONSISTENT SELECTORS —

On the 1951–52 tour to the British Isles and France, the selectors used only 17 players in the five tests, the smallest number ever. In the 1938 series against the British Lions the selectors used only 18 players. In the 1970 series against New Zealand the selectors also used only 18 players, one being a substitute when Robbie Barnard from Transvaal replaced Piston van Wyk in the second test at Newlands.

— SPRINGBOKS NOT BORN IN SOUTH AFRICA —

Quite a few Springboks have been born in the United Kingdom, and our neighbouring country Zimbabwe (formerly Rhodesia) has also produced its fair share. Zambia, in southern Africa, produced three Springboks: the McCallum brothers, Ian and Roy, as well as Springbok captain Corné Krige.

The list of Springboks not born in South Africa is:

Name	Birthplace	Country	Caps	Career
Frank Guthrie	Notting Hill, London	England	3	1891-96
Edward Little	Midlothian	Scotland	2	1891
Bob Snedden	Kirkgate	Scotland	1	1891
Edward Trenery	Hayle, Cornwall	England	1	1891
Charlie Chignell	Heavitree, Devon	England	1	1891
Ferdy Aston	Cheltenham	England	4	1896
Henry Gorton	Burton Extra	England	1	1896
Ernest Olver	Liskeard, Cornwall	England	1	1896
Ben Andrew	Hey, Lancashire	England	1	1896
HH Forbes	Mt Ararat, Victoria	Australia	1	1896
Alf Larard	Kingston-upon-Hull	England	2	1896
Tommy Etlinger	London	England	1	1896
Tommy Hepburn	Shoshong	Bechuanaland	1	1896
Herman van Broekhuizen	Ryse	Netherlands	1	1896
Alexander Frew	Kilmarnock	Scotland	1	1903
Willie McEwan	Edinburgh	Scotland	2	1903
JEC Partridge	Llanthewy Skirrid	Wales	1	1903
George Crampton	Aughrim	Ireland	1	1903
Hugh Ferris	Newry, Co Down	Ireland	1	1903
Taffy Townsend	Newport	Wales	1	1921
Geoff Gray	Hastings	England	4	1931–33
Des van Jaarsveldt	Bulawayo	Rhodesia	1	1960
Ian McCallum	K'Kana	Zambia	11	1970–74
Roy McCallum	Kitwe	Zambia	1	1974
Ian Robertson	Salisbury	Rhodesia	5	1974–76

Name	Birthplace	Country	Caps	Career
David Smith	Bulawayo	Rhodesia	4	1980
Chris Rogers	Bulawayo	Rhodesia	4	1984
Nick Mallett	Haileybury	England	2	1984
John Allan	Glasgow	Scotland	13	1993–96
Steve Atherton	Gosport	England	8	1993–96
Gary Teichmann	Gwelo	Rhodesia	42	1995–99
Adrian Garvey	Bulawayo	Rhodesia	28	1996–99
Bob Skinstad	Bulawayo	Rhodesia	42	1997–2007
Christian Stewart	Toronto	Canada	3	1998
Corné Krige	Lusaka	Zambia	39	1999–2003
Christo Bezuidenhout	Canary Islands	Spain	4	2003
Tonderai Chavhanga	Masvingo	Zimbabwe	4	2005–08
Brian Mujati	Bulawayo	Zimbabwe	12	2008
Tendai Mtawarira	Harare	Zimbabwe	10	2008–09

— NEVER ON A SATURDAY —

South Africa's first international in 1891 took place on a Thursday, and the same happened in 1896. There doesn't appear to be a specific reason for this, the only logical explanation being that in those days Saturday was a working day just like the rest of the week and it was thought they might get more spectators on a Thursday. During the Rugby World Cup in 1995, 1999, 2003 and 2007, many games did not take place on Saturdays because of limited time in the tournament.

The list of test matches not played on a Saturday are:

In South Africa

Thursday 30 July 1891, first test against Great Britain, Crusader Ground, Port Elizabeth.

Thursday 30 July 1896, first test against Great Britain, Crusader Ground, Port Elizabeth.

Wednesday 26 August 1903, first test against Great Britain, Old Wanderers, Johannesburg.

Thursday 13 April 1995, against Western Samoa, Ellis Park, Johannesburg.
Thursday 25 May 1995, against Australia, Newlands, Cape Town.
Thursday 30 May 1995, against Romania, Newlands, Cape Town.
Tuesday 2 July 1996, against Fiji, Loftus Versfeld, Pretoria.
Tuesday 10 June 1997, against Tonga, Newlands, Cape Town.
Wednesday 15 August 2007, against Namibia, Newlands, Cape Town.

Abroad
Friday 25 September 1981, against the USA, Owl Creek Polo Field, Glenville.
Sunday 3 October 1999, against Scotland, Murrayfield, Edinburgh.
Sunday 10 October 1999, against Spain, Murrayfield, Edinburgh.
Friday 15 October 1999, against Uruguay, Hampden Park, Glasgow.
Sunday 24 October 1999, against England, Stade de France, Paris.
Thursday 4 November 1999, against New Zealand, Millennium Stadium, Cardiff.
Sunday 12 November 2000, against Argentina, River Plate Stadium, Buenos Aires.
Sunday 19 November 2000, against Ireland, Lansdowne Road, Dublin.
Sunday 26 November 2000, against Wales, Millennium Stadium, Cardiff.
Friday 24 October 2003, against Georgia, Stadium Australia, Sydney.
Sunday 9 September 2007, against Samoa, Parc des Princes, Paris.
Friday 14 September 2007, against England, Stade de France, St. Denis.
Sunday 30 September 2007, against the USA, Stade de la Mosson, Montpellier.
Sunday 7 October 2007, against Fiji, Stade Velodrome, Marseilles.
Sunday, 14 October 2007, against Argentina, Stade de France, St Denis.

— FLOODLIGHTS —

The first floodlit game involving South Africa was the touring fixture against Aquitaine at the Stade du Hameau in Pau on 7 October 1992, which the Springboks won 29–22. The first test to start under lights was the second test against France at Ellis Park, Johannesburg on 3 July 1993, with the visitors winning a thriller 18–17.

— CLOSED ROOF —

South Africa's first game under a closed roof was at Colonial Stadium, Melbourne on 8 July 2000 when Australia won 44–23.

Date	Venue	Opponents	Result
8 July 2000	Colonial Stadium, Melbourne	Australia	Lost 23–44
22 Nov 2000	Millennium Stadium, Cardiff	Wales A	Won 34–15
8 Nov 2003	Colonial Stadium, Melbourne	New Zealand	Lost 9–29
24 Nov 2007	Millennium Stadium, Cardiff	Wales	Won 34–12
8 Nov 2008	Millennium Stadium, Cardiff	Wales	Won 20–15
13 Nov 2010	Millennium Stadium, Cardiff	Wales	Won 29–25

— SPRINGBOK LEGENDS: JAN ELLIS —

JAN ELLIS FACTFILE
Born: 5 January 1942 in Brakpan, Transvaal
Provinces: South West Africa, Transvaal
Caps: 38 (W22, D6, L10)
Scoring: 21 points (7 tries)
Springbok debut: vs New Zealand on 31 July 1965

Jan Ellis in typical fashion, running with the ball in one hand.

Jan Hendrik Ellis was born in the Transvaal but lived in South West Africa since childhood. He made his first-class debut for South West Africa (now Namibia) on 12 June 1962 against the British Lions at lock, but his rugby career for South West Africa had been turbulent and controversial. Bluntly outspoken, he was often at loggerheads with the selectors and rugby administrators and they, in turn, struck back by not considering him for the provincial side on several occasions. That is why he only played in 50 games for his province from 1962 to 1974.

He made his international debut in 1965 on the disastrous tour to New Zealand, but played in all four tests. In the 1967 series against France, Ellis and Piet Greyling began the flank partnership that lasted for 25 tests. It was generally regarded that they formed the best combination in world rugby at the time. Ellis and Greyling complemented each other perfectly. From the start of the partnership Greyling fitted naturally into the less spectacular but no less effective tighter role, leaving the faster, more powerful Ellis to do the roving. They reached their peak against the 1970 All Blacks. Fit, fast and fearless, they controlled the loose ball and completely disrupted the All Black's pattern. Jan Ellis scored 32 tries for the Springboks in 74 matches (7 tries in 38 tests) but the most spectacular of the 32 tries was the one he scored against the Barbarians in the last game of the 1969–70 tour in the United Kingdom. This try is described by Chris Greyvensten: 'Twelve minutes to go and the ball rolls loose 40 metres from the Barbarians' goal. Swooping down on it is Jan Ellis, the red-haired flank from South West Africa. The ball is scooped up in one easy-flowing, almost casual, movement and then he is off in that loping, long striding run of his. Two defenders are brushed aside with a flip of the shoulder and a sway of the hips. Another one is beaten with an all but imperceptible change of pace. Now the ball is clutched in one big, freckled hand and running with perfect balance on the soft green turf, Ellis sidesteps free of the cover defence with only Mike Gibson, Ireland's outstanding centre, between him and the try-line. A feint as if to pass and Gibson goes the wrong way as Ellis thunders past him to score one of the greatest tries in the history of international rugby without a finger being laid on him on his weaving 40 metre run.'

Ellis's seven tries equalled the record of Ferdie Bergh for a forward, and was the record until Mark Andrews broke it in 1997. He also equalled Frik du Preez's record of 38 test matches for South Africa in 1976 and this was the record until it was surpassed by James Small in 1997.

— WHAT'S IN A NAME —

Gerhard Hamilton Brand was born in Cape Town on 8 October 1906 and grew up in a family where rugby was a major interest. In fact, his father was a member of the Hamilton Rugby Club at the time. It was his grandfather who suggested that his second Christian name should be Hamilton in honour of the Rugby Club. It is rather fitting that Brand played for this club throughout his career.

'Fairy' Heatlie, the first South African captain to lead a winning team, and a man that played a big role in establishing rugby in Argentina (he played in one test for Argentina in 1910), was actually christened Barry Heatlie Heatlie. He was born on the farm Glen Heatlie in the district of Worcester on 25 April 1872.

— GEFFIN, JUST GEFFIN —

It is an interesting fact that Okey Geffin must be the only Springbok never to have had an official first name. Everybody accepted it to be Aaron, but there was nothing but a blank space on his birth certificate until he had it rectified years later. Okey has always had his own explanation for this. 'When my father went to register my birth and they asked him for my Christian names, he must have said: "He's a Jewish boy! He's got no Christian names!" And years later it cost me R30 to make it official that I am Aaron Okey Geffin!'

— CHANGED THEIR NAMES —

Basie Vivier never changed his surname from Viviers to Vivier as many people believe. The fact is that his surname has always been simply Vivier, but that journalists always wrote it incorrectly with the 's' at the end.

Hubert Gordon (Bert) Reid (1906–07) had to change his surname to Botha-Reid before he could marry the daughter of Louis Botha, Prime Minister of South Africa from 1910 to 1919.

Johannes Haindly Joseph (Bolla) Conradie always left out the Joseph in his names until it was discovered in 2007 that the actually has a third name.

Justin Stefan (Justin) Swart always left out the Stefan. Professor Piet van der Schyff, the Historian of the SA Rugby Union, discovered this when he wrote a book about Paul Roos Gymnasium, the school that Swart attended in Stellenbosch.

— BENCHED BUT NO TEST CAP —

The following players sat on the bench for the Springboks but didn't get a chance to come on, and never gained a full test cap for South Africa:

Name	Province	Year	Matches
Ronnie Potgieter	Northern Transvaal	1970	1
Daan Ackermann *	Western Transvaal	1970	1
Chris Luther *	Northern Transvaal	1972	1
Gert Schutte *	Griquas	1972–77	4

Name	Province	Year	Matches
Gavin Cowley *	Eastern Province	1974–76	3
Malcolm Swanby *	Natal	1974	2
Corrie Pypers *	Transvaal	1977	1
Tim Cocks	Natal	1980–81	8
Gawie Visagie	Natal	1981	2
Shaun Povey	Western Province	1981	4
John Robbie *	Transvaal	1984	4
Liaan Kirkham *	Transvaal	1984	2
André Skinner *	Northern Transvaal	1984	2
Wessel Lightfoot *	Free State	1984	2
Schalk Naudé *	Transvaal	1986	4
Donovan Twiname *	Northern Transvaal	1986	2
André Markgraaff *	South West Africa	1986	2
Andrew Paterson *	Western Province	1989	2
Harry Roberts	Transvaal	1992	5
Deon Oosthuysen	Northern Transvaal	1992	1
Botha Rossouw	Western Transvaal	1992	1
Piet Pretorius	Northern Transvaal	1992	1
Hentie Martens	Free State	1993	2
FA Meiring	Northern Transvaal	1994	1
Japie Barnard *	Northern Transvaal	1994	1
Jannie Claassens	Northern Transvaal	1994	4
Lance Sherrell	Northern Transvaal	1994	2
Tinus Linee	Western Province	1994	1
Kevin Putt	Natal	1994	8
Joggie Viljoen	Western Province	1996	1
Boeta Wessels	Griquas	1997	3
Joe Gillingham	Transvaal	1997	1
Steven Sykes	Sharks	2009	1

* Never gained Springbok colours

— WARMING THE BENCH —

Werner Swanepoel sat out a staggering total of 23 complete tests on the replacements bench without getting on to the park, but at least found time to gain 20 caps (12 as a starter) between 1997 and 2000.

The most selections on the bench without ever winning a full cap is held by Tim Cocks and Kevin Putt, with eight selections apiece.

— NO CAPS! —

There are only two occasions when a South African team took the field with no test experience: the first-ever test against the British Isles on 30 July 1891, and against New Zealand on 16 July 1949, South Africa's first test since 1938 because of the Second World War.

— BEFORE AND AFTER THE WAR —

Two players, Boy and Gerhard Morkel, played for South Africa both before and after the First World War. The only Springbok player from 1938 who was still playing provincial rugby in 1949 was Jan Lotz. Dr Danie Craven writes the following in his book *Springbok Story 1949–1953*: 'There is no doubt that if the All Blacks had come out in 1948 as originally planned, Jan Lotz would have been in the side.'

— THE WELLINGTON MONK —

On 23 July 1921 a monk played for Wellington against the Springboks under an assumed name. An ordained priest, Reverend Father Paul Kane, SM, named as Paul Markham of Marist Old Boys in the team sheet, lined up in the backs and played the whole game in a 3–8 defeat at Athletic Park.

— ODD JOBS —

In the professional era there are few rugby players who have another career, but in the past, as amateur players, they were drawn from a variety of professions:

Springbok farmers

Philip Nel
Ebbo Bastard
Tommy Laubscher
Henry Honiball
Os du Randt

Springboks in the medical profession

Jan Stegmann
PK Albertyn
Jack van Druten
Louis Babrow
Ernst Dinkelmann
Colin Kroon
Attie Baard
Gert Brynard
Corra Dirksen
Piet de Wet
Cecil Moss
Alan Menter
Ian McCallum
Roy McCallum
Chris Pope
Derek van den Berg
Edrich Krantz
Christo Wagenaar
Daan du Plessis
Divan Serfontein
Michael du Plessis
Uli Schmidt
Brendan Venter
Jannie du Plessis
Johann Styger

Springboks with doctorates

Herman van Broekhuizen
Gideon Roos
Danie Craven
Johan Claassen
Piet Goosen
Hannes Marais
John Williams

Pierre Edwards
Jan du Preez
Ben du Toit

Springboks in the pulpit
Herman van Broekhuizen
Koot Reynecke
George Daneel
Anton Stegmann
André McDonald
'Snowy' Suter
Ben-Piet van Zyl
Dawie de Villiers
Darius Botha

Springboks on the bench
Percy Jones (Judge in the Cape Provincial Division of the Supreme Court: 1926-46; Judge President 1946)

— MILESTONE TRIES —

The Springboks have scored more than a 1 000 tries since Theo Samuels claimed their first in 1896 after South Africa had failed to score a single try against Great Britain in 1891. Johannesburg was a happy hunting ground for South Africa in the early years with the first, the 100th and the 200th test tries scored in this city; the first milestone at the Old Wanderers Ground, and the latter two at Ellis Park. The honour of scoring South Africa's 1 000th test try belongs to JP Pietersen when he dotted down against Fiji in the 2007 Rugby World Cup.

Here is a list of players scoring milestone tries in South African rugby:

Try	Name	Date	Opponent	Venue
1	Theo Samuels	22 Aug 1896	British Isles	Johannesburg
50	Attie van Heerden	13 Aug 1921	New Zealand	Dunedin
100	Fanie Louw	6 Aug 1938	British Isles	Johannesburg
200	John Gainsford	5 Aug 1961	Australia	Johannesburg
300	Gerrie Germishuys	24 Jul 1976	New Zealand	Durban

Try	Name	Date	Opponent	Venue
400	Tiaan Strauss	14 Nov 1992	England	Twickenham
500	Penalty try	9 Nov 1996	Argentina	Buenos Aires
600	Gary Teichmann	20 Jun 1998	Ireland	Pretoria
700	Werner Swanepoel	8 Jul 2000	Australia	Melbourne
800	Bakkies Botha	11 Oct 2003	Uruguay	Perth
900	Percy Montgomery	5 Nov 2005	Argentina	Buenos Aires
1 000	JP Pietersen	7 Oct 2007	Fiji	Marseilles
1 100	Gurthrö Steenkamp	28 Aug 2010	Australia	Pretoria

— SPRINGBOK NUMBERS —

Milestones of Springbok players in all games, including tests and touring matches:

No	Name	Province	Date (Opponents)
1	Ben Duff	Western Province	30 Jul 1891 (Great Britain)
100	Douglas Brooks	Border	24 Oct 1906 (Middlesex)
200	Hennie Potgieter	Orange Free State	30 Jun 1928 (New Zealand)
300	Ernst Dinkelmann	Northern Transvaal	10 Oct 1951 (South Eastern Counties)
400	Dirk de Vos	Western Province	6 Apr 1965 (Combined Universities)
500	Willie du Plessis	Western Province	26 Apr 1980 (South America)
600	Ollie le Roux	Free State	30 Oct 1993 (Buenos Aires)
700	Craig Davidson	Natal	15 Nov 2000 (Ireland A)
800	Adriaan Strauss	Free State	19 Jul 2008 (Australia)

— SPRINGBOK TEST NUMBERS —

Milestones of Springbok players in all test matches:

No	Name	Province	Date (Opponents)
1	Ben Duff	Western Province	30 Jul 1891 (Great Britain)
100	Anton Stegmann	Western Province	17 Nov 1906 (Scotland)
200	Alvi van der Merwe	Western Province	5 Dec 1931 (Wales)
300	James Starke	Western Province	1 Sep 1956 (New Zealand)
400	Hannes Viljoen	Natal	17 Jul 1971 (Australia)
500	Robert du Preez	Natal	15 Aug 1992 (New Zealand)
600	Wayne Julies	Boland	10 Oct 1999 (Spain)
700	Tendai Mtawarira	Natal	14 Jun 2008 (Wales)

— CENTRES GALORE —

When Heinke van der Merwe received a call-up to the Springbok squad in 2006 on their Tri-Nations tour in Australia and New Zealand, he became the fifth Springbok produced by Monument High School in Krugersdorp, but he was the first non-centre. Christo Wagenaar (1977), Brendan Venter (1994-99), Jorrie Muller (2003) and Jaque Fourie (2003–2010) are the other Monnas Springboks. In 2010 Willem Alberts (Flanker) became the sixth Monument High School Springbok, scoring a try from the bench in his first three tests.

— WATT DISMISSES 'THE DON' – TWICE —

Howard Watt, the 1937 Springbok to Australia and New Zealand who died in 2005, was the last surviving pre-war Springbok. He was also a cricketer who represented Western Province and North-East Transvaal in the Currie Cup as a fast bowler before he made his rugby debut in 1935.

In 1928 he moved to Chicago and in July 1932 an Australian team including the legendary Don Bradman toured the USA and Canada. The Australians played a series of four one-day games on successive days at Grant Park in Chicago against an Illinois XI. Watt played in each match and dismissed the great man twice, for just 4 runs on 23 July and for 13 two days later.

When Watt met Bradman again in 1937, Bradman remembered him as one of the few people to dismiss him so cheaply. Bradman also signed a ball for him and Watt later donated it to the Western Province Cricket Association.

— THE USA TOUR —

In 1981, after the tour to New Zealand, the Springboks were scheduled to play three games in the United States of America, including one international against the American Eagles. The first game against a Midwest side took place on Saturday, 19 September at Roosevelt Park in Racine, Wisconsin at 09h15, the only time a Springbok side ever played a game in the morning. There was drama before the second game at the Bleecker Stadium in Albany when the Governor of New York, Hugh Carey, applied for a court order to prevent the game from taking place, but the High Court ruled against it and the match against an Eastern Rugby Union side eventually did go ahead.

The test match against the United States Eagles was also scheduled for the Bleecker Stadium for Saturday, 26 September. Because of security concerns the Springbok tour management, together with the chairman of the Eastern Rugby Union, Tom Selfridge, decided to schedule the game for the Friday afternoon. The time and venue for the game was kept secret from all except the players, reserves and a handful of officials from both sides. The Springboks who were not selected for the game were also kept in the dark about where and when the fixture would take place. The President of the American Rugby Union, David Chambers, was on an aeroplane on his way to New York when the game kicked off at the Owl Creek Polo Field in Glenville, New York state.

Thys Burger, who was one of the Springbok reserves, assisted in erecting the set of poles just before the match, and he was then invited to act as touch judge. When Theuns Stofberg left the field just before halftime, he was replaced by the self-same Burger. Burger, in turn, was substituted as touch judge by another Springbok reserve, Gysie Pienaar. To end his busy and versatile afternoon, Burger also scored a try – the first Springbok substitute to do so. Edrich Krantz, who was earlier in the morning requested by the tour management to buy a few gifts for their American hosts, returned to the hotel just as the Springbok team left for the test. He also attended the test – the only Springbok not directly involved in the match to do so. After the game Herman le Roux, the rugby writer who covered the tour for Nasionale Pers and who, like all the other hacks on tour, was kept in the dark about the fixture, had the brainwave of asking Krantz (a medical doctor by profession and who, like Le Roux, hailed from Bloemfontein in the Free State) to write a report of the game. Krantz promptly obliged. On the team's return to South Africa, Alex Kellermann, the then secretary of the South African Rugby Board, confronted Le Roux about the latter's decision to let a player write a report. After Le Roux had convinced Kellermann that Krantz did not receive any payment for writing the report, the issue was laid to rest.

For the record, South Africa won 38–7, and later Quintus van Rooyen, editor of the *SA Rugby Annual*, reported the attendance as '35 spectators, twenty policeman, one television crew, one reporter and no demonstrators'.

— SPRINGBOK COACHES —

Name	Tenure	P	W	D	L
Danie Craven	1949–56	23	17	–	6
Basil Kenyon	1958	2	–	1	1
Hennie Muller	1960–61, 1963, 1965	17	8	1	8
Boy Louw	1960–61, 1965	13	6	1	6
Izak van Heerden	1962	4	3	–	1
Felix du Plessis	1964	2	1	–	1
Ian Kirkpatrick	1967, 1974	6	4	1	1
Avril Malan	1969–70	8	4	2	2
Johan Claassen	1964, 1968, 1970–74	22	13	2	7
Nelie Smith	1980–81	15	12	–	3
Cecil Moss	1982–89	11	9	–	2
John Williams	1992	5	1	–	4
Gerrie Sonnekus	1993[1]	–	–	–	–
Ian McIntosh	1993–94	12	4	2	6
Kitch Christie	1994–95	14	14	–	–
André Markgraaff	1996	13	8	–	5
Carel du Plessis	1997	8	3	–	5
Nick Mallett	1997–2000	38	27	–	11

Name	Tenure	P	W	D	L
Harry Viljoen	2000–01	15	8	1	6
Rudolf Straeuli	2002–03	23	12	–	11
Jake White	2004–07	54	36	1	17
Peter de Villiers	2008 – present	39	25	–	14

[1] Did not take up the position.

— SPRINGBOK SELECTORS —

Bill Schreiner holds the distinction of being a South African selector from 1912 to 1951, from 1921 as the Chairman. He was a son of the third President of the SA Rugby Board, Bill Schreiner (1913–15).

Here's a full list of selectors, with the dates when change(s) were made:

1903: Barry Heatlie, Percy Jones, Biddy Anderson.[1]
1906: Jim Crosby, Clarrie Becker, JD Hedden, A Solomon, CJ van Renen, C Waymouth.
1910: 'Daddy' Carden, Percy Day, Percy Jones, AB Lawton, Japie Louw, Stanton.[2]
1910: 'Daddy' Carden, Percy Day, JD Heddon, AB Lawton, Percy Jones, Stanton.[3]
1910: 'Daddy' Carden, Percy Day, Percy Jones, AB Lawton, Japie Louw.[4]
1912: G Stack, AB Lawton, HC Bennett, George St Leger Devenish, Bill Schreiner.
1921: Bill Schreiner, SA Townsend, J Leck, 'Mark' Markötter, Clarrie Bekker.
1924: Bill Schreiner, SA Townsend, George St Leger Devenish, 'Mark' Markötter, 'Uncle' Dobbin.
1928: Bill Schreiner, SA Townsend, George St Leger Devenish, 'Mark' Markötter, Theo Pienaar.
1933: Bill Schreiner, SA Townsend, George St Leger Devenish, 'Mark' Markötter, PL Kriek.
1937: Bill Schreiner, George St Leger Devenish, 'Mark' Markötter, Frank Mellish, Arthur Barlow.
1938: Bill Schreiner, SA Townsend, George St Leger Devenish, 'Mark' Markötter, Bill Zeller.
1949: Bill Schreiner, Frank Mellish, Bill Zeller, Danie Craven, Bert Kipling.

1951: Bill Schreiner, Frank Mellish, Bill Zeller, Geoff Gray, Bert Kipling.
1953: Frank Mellish, Bill Zeller, Danie Craven, Geoff Gray, Bert Kipling.
1955: Frank Mellish, Bill Zeller, Danie Craven, Basil Kenyon, Morris Zimerman.
1956: Frank Mellish, Bill Zeller, Danie Craven, Basil Kenyon, Jan Lotz.
1958: Frank Mellish, Basil Kenyon, Morris Zimerman, Jan Lotz, George van Reenen.
1961: Frank Mellish, Morris Zimerman, Jan Lotz, George van Reenen, Gerry Brand.
1963: George van Reenen, Morris Zimerman, Jan Lotz, Gerry Brand, Johan Claassen.
1964: Frank Mellish, Morris Zimerman, Jan Lotz, Gerry Brand, Boy Louw.
1965: Morris Zimerman, Basil Kenyon, Jan Lotz, Boy Louw, Flappie Lochner.
1966: Flappie Lochner, Basil Kenyon, Johan Claassen, Ian Kirkpatrick, PA Malan.
1967: Flappie Lochner, Johan Claassen, Ian Kirkpatrick, Boy Louw, Morris Zimerman.
1969: Flappie Lochner, Johan Claassen, Ian Kirkpatrick, Tjol Lategan, Avril Malan.
1970: Flappie Lochner, Johan Claassen, Ian Kirkpatrick, Avril Malan, Daan Swiegers.
1971: Johan Claassen, Ian Kirkpatrick, Daan Swiegers, Nelie Smith, Dave Stewart.
1972: Johan Claassen, Ian Kirkpatrick, Butch Lochner, Daan Swiegers, Nelie Smith.
1977: Butch Lochner, Ian Kirkpatrick, Daan Swiegers, Nelie Smith, Brian Irvine.
1978: Butch Lochner, Ian Kirkpatrick, Daan Swiegers, Nelie Smith, Brian Irvine, Arthur Dwesi, Dougie Dyers.
1980: Butch Lochner, Brian Irvine, Ian Kirkpatrick, Nelie Smith, Daan Swiegers, Arthur Dwesi, Dougie Dyers.
1981: Butch Lochner, Brian Irvine, Ian Kirkpatrick, Daan Swiegers, Nelie Smith, EM Mboya, Dougie Dyers.
1982: Daan Swiegers, Nic Bojé, Dougie Dyers, Brian Irvine, Hannes Marais, Cecil Moss, John September.
1984: Daan Swiegers, Cecil Moss, Nic Bojé, Hannes Marais, Abie Malan, Dougie Dyers, John September.

1985: Daan Swiegers, Dougie Dyers, Nic Bojé, Cecil Moss, John September, Abie Malan, Wynand Claassen.
1986: Daan Swiegers, Dougie Dyers, Abie Malan, Hannes Marais, Cecil Moss, John September, Barry Wolmarans.
1988: Daan Swiegers, Dougie Dyers, Abie Malan, Hannes Marais, John September, Barry Wolmarans.
1989: Daan Swiegers, Dougie Dyers, Abie Malan, Hannes Marais, Cecil Moss, John September, Barry Wolmarans.
1990: Daan Swiegers, Dougie Dyers, Hannes Marais, John September, Abie Malan, Barry Wolmarans.
1991: Daan Swiegers, Mickey Gerber, Hannes Marais, John September, Dawie Snyman, C Williams, John Williams.
1992: Daan Swiegers, Jackie Abrahams, Bill Jardine, Abie Malan, John Williams, Vuyisile Zwelibanzi.
1993: Daan Swiegers, Jackie Abrahams, Bill Jardine, Ian McIntosh, Vuyisile Zwelibanzi.
1994: Kitch Christie, Dougie Dyers, Hannes Marais.
1995: Kitch Christie, Hannes Marais, Gysie Pienaar.
1996: André Markgraaff, François Davids, Mickey Gerber.
1997: Mickey Gerber, Carel du Plessis, François Davids
1998: Nick Mallett, Mickey Gerber, François Davids
2001: François Davids, Harry Viljoen, Wynand Claassen
2002: François Davids, Harry Viljoen, Wynand Claassen
2004: André Markgraaff, Pieter Jooste, Jake White
2005: Ian McIntosh, Peter Jooste, Jake White
2006: Pieter Jooste, Ian McIntosh, Jake White
2008: Pieter Jooste, Ian McIntosh, Peter de Villiers

Note: The first name is always the chairman/convenor.

Note: Prior to 1906 the international match centre appointed a selection team to select the South African team.

1. Only for the last test at Newlands, Cape Town.
2. Only for the first test at the Old Wanderers, Johannesburg.
3. Only for the second test at the Crusader Ground, Port Elizabeth.
4. Only for the third test at Newlands, Cape Town.

— LATE STARTERS —

Two Springbok matches at the 1995 World Cup in South Africa started late for different reasons:

The game against Canada in Port Elizabeth on 3 June started 45 minutes late because of a power failure which affected the floodlights.

The semi-final match versus France in Durban on 17 June began 90 minutes late because of a waterlogged ground after unseasonal torrential rain in Natal. The whole match was played in incessant rain.

— SCOTTISH AFFAIR —

When the Great Britain side toured South Africa in 1903, the first test match was played at the Old Wanderers in Johannesburg on Wednesday, 26 August. By sheer coincidence the British captain was a Scot, Mark Morrison, and the South African captain, Alex Frew, was also a Scot. Amazingly enough, the referee, WP (Bill) Donaldson was also Scottish, having played for his native land from 1893 to 1899. Perhaps it just worked out that way or maybe Bill Donaldson was being diplomatic, but the result of the match was a draw, 10–10.

For many years it was believed that the same Dr Alex Frew only played provincial rugby in South Africa for Transvaal. However, according to information in the book about Griqualand West, written by Frikkie van Rensburg in 1986, a certain Dr J Frew played in one game for Griquas in 1902. Hannes Kotze from Bloemfontein, a collector of autographs and photos of all Springboks from 1891, discovered a team photo of Pirates Rugby Club in Kimberley in 1902, and Dr Alex Frew appears on the photo. The Frew that played for Griquas in 1902 was indeed Dr Alex Frew. Dr Danie Craven writes in his book *The Legends of Springbok Rugby 1889-1989*: 'Frew had come to South Africa in 1902 to take up an appointment at the Orange River Station Refugee Camp, situated between Bloemfontein and Prieska. The name refugee camp was in fact a euphemism for its proper name – concentration camp.'

— SOUTH AFRICA'S RECORD CAP HOLDER —

Percy Montgomery is South Africa's leading cap winner of all time, overtaking Joost van der Westhuizen in 2007, while Frik du Preez was the leading cap winner for 26 years from 1971 until James Small took the record in 1997.

Here's the complete list of all the holders of the record:

Record holder	New record established
Barry Heatlie	5th cap – 26 Aug 1903
Bob Loubser	7th cap – 3 Sep 1910
'Uncle' Dobbin	8th cap – 30 Nov 1912
Phil Mostert	10th cap – 1 Sep 1928
Bennie Osler	15th cap – 12 Aug 1933
Boy Louw	18th cap – 10 Sep 1938
Salty du Rand	19th cap – 4 Aug 1956
Chris Koch	22nd cap – 23 Jul 1960
Johan Claassen	23rd cap – 5 Aug 1961
John Gainsford	29th cap – 4 Sep 1965
Frik du Preez	34th cap – 12 Jun 1971
Jan Ellis	38th cap – 24 July 1976 (equalled record)
James Small	39th cap – 19 Jul 1997
Mark Andrews	48th cap – 15 Aug 1998
Joost van der Westhuizen	62nd cap – 8 Jul 2000
Mark Andrews	71st cap – 30 Jun 2001
Joost van der Westhuizen	77th cap – 17 Nov 2001
Percy Montgomery	90th cap – 22 Sep 2007
John Smit	102nd cap – 4 Sep 2010
Victor Matfield	103rd cap – 13 Nov 2010

— SPRINGBOK LEGENDS: NAAS BOTHA —

NAAS BOTHA FACTFILE
Born: 27 February 1958 in Breyten, South Eastern Transvaal
Province: Northern Transvaal
Caps: 28 (W19, D0, L9)
Scoring: 2 tries, 50 conversions, 50 penalties and 18 dropped goals – 312 points
Springbok debut: 26 April 1980 vs South America (Wanderers, Johannesburg)

Naas Botha kicks, and it's three points on the board.

The blond Northern Transvaal flyhalf Hendrik Egnatius Botha made his international debut in 1980 against the touring South Americans on 26 April 1980, exactly three years to the day after he made his provincial debut at the age of 19 for Northern Transvaal against South Eastern Transvaal in 1977. Regarded by many as the greatest match-winner in world rugby, Dr Danie Craven described him as 'a genius – a match-winner, I've often said it, and I'll say it again: I cannot believe that a team with Naas Botha in its ranks could ever lose a match'. Because of the isolation years in South African rugby, Botha only played in 28 tests from 1980 to 1992, scoring 312 points. Only Percy Montgomery has scored more points for South Africa in test matches. Botha also kicked an amazing 18 dropped goals in tests which is still the South African record. He is the brother of another Springbok, Darius Botha. Captain of South Africa in 9 tests from 1986 to 1992, Naas also holds the South African first-class points total record with 3 781 points in 277 matches. He was the SA Rugby player of the year in 1979, 1981, 1985 and 1987. Botha spent a lot of time abroad, scoring 1 731 points for Rovigo in Italy from 1987 to 1993, playing in four Italian Championship finals, and gaining two winners' medals in 1989 and 1990. He was awarded Provincial colours in softball and baseball, and even became an American football player in 1983, but returned to South Africa and was reinstated as an amateur. Naas scored 1 699 Currie Cup points for Northern Transvaal, which is still the South African record for the most points by a player.

— SOUTH AFRICA'S RECORD CAREER POINTS SCORER —

The honour of being South Africa's leading all-time points scorer has been held for the last seven years by Percy Montgomery, who passed Naas Botha's old mark in 2004 after Botha had himself held the record for 23 years. Gerry Brand held the record for the longest time – 25 years – between 1938 and 1963.

Record-holder	New record established
Theo Samuels	6 pts – 29 Aug 1896
Bob Loubser	9 pts – 1 Dec 1906
Duggie Morkel	14 pts – 3 Sep 1910
Bennie Osler	40 pts – 8 Jul 1933

Record-holder	New record established
Gerry Brand	55 pts – 6 Aug 1938
Keith Oxlee	61 pts – 13 Jul 1963
Piet Visagie	71 pts – 16 Aug 1969
Naas Botha	134 pts – 29 Aug 1991
Percy Montgomery	319 pts – 24 Jul 2004

— SOUTH AFRICA'S RECORD CAREER TRY SCORER —

Joost van der Westhuizen is South Africa's joint leading try scorer (along with Bryan Habana) in tests with 38, but he first claimed that record a decade ago with his 21st try to surpass James Small. The longest spell as the Springbok all-time leading try scorer is 38 years by Ferdie Bergh until John Gainsford scored his 8th try on 4 September 1965.

— INJURED REFS —

There were four occasions when a referee of a test that the Springboks were involved in had to be replaced due to injury:

Date	Opponent	Referee	Replaced by	Min
30 Nov 1912	Ireland (Dublin)	JT Tulloch	Fred Gardiner	41
4 Sep 1965	NZ (Christchurch)	Pat Murphy	Alan Taylor	21
24 Nov 2001	England (Twickenham)	Stuart Dickinson	David McHugh	12
10 Aug 2002	NZ (Durban)	David McHugh	Chris White	42

JT Tulloch could not go on because of a twisted ankle.
Pat Murphy was replaced because of a hamstring injury.
Stuart Dickinson left the field because of a pulled calf muscle.
David McHugh dislocated his shoulder when a spectator, Piet van Zyl, ran onto the field and tackled McHugh. Van Zyl was banned from all rugby for life.

— TWO-TEST SERIES —

The Springboks have won 28 of the 36 two-test series they have contested, with 25 of those by a score of two wins to nil. They have lost just three two-game series – against France in 1958 and 1993 and in Australia (with the only two-nil scoreline) in 1965.

— THREE-TEST SERIES —

South Africa have won five and lost five of the ten three-test series they have contested. The only clean sweep of victories was in Australia in 1971, and the only time the Springboks were whitewashed was in their very first series against Great Britain in 1891.

South Africa have just once lost the opening game of a three-test rubber but won the series – in New Zealand in 1937, while the only time that they won the opening test but lost the series was in Australia in 1993.

— FOUR-TEST SERIES —

South Africa's record in four-match rubbers is won 12, drawn 3, lost 4, with two of those series victories – against New Zealand in 1949 and Australia in 1969 – being a whitewash.

Incidentally, the Boks have never managed to win a series in which they lost the opening test, or lose a series in which they won the opening game.

— SPRINGBOKS GO GREEN —

In South Africa's early test appearances the team was not only selected by a committee of people from the home city, but the team wore the club jersey of a local club. In the fourth and final test against Great Britain in 1896, the Springboks wore green jerseys for the first time when their captain, Barry Heatlie, brought the olive green colours of his club, the Old Diocesans College, and South Africa were rewarded with a first-ever victory.

In the third and final test on 12 September 1903 against the British Isles in Cape Town, Heatlie was recalled to the team and made captain once more. By this time the Old Diocesan club had ceased to exist but the outfitters still had supplies of the club kit. South Africa duly took to the field in green shirts with white collars, black shorts and red socks borrowed from the Villagers club. The Springboks won the game and their first series victory.

On 12 September 1906, three years to the day later, the South African board settled on these colours for their tour to the United Kingdom.

In the third test against New Zealand in 1928 in Port Elizabeth the Springboks wore white shorts for the first time, the only reason being that it was easier for referee VH (Boet) Neser to identify the two teams. By 1937 the shorts were changed to white, the collars became old gold, and the socks green. For the 1938 visit to Britain, the Springboks temporarily reverted to black shorts, but it was short-lived, and white became the favoured colour, and remains so. Early colours were:

1891
1st test – Crusader club jersey (white), Port Elizabeth
2nd test – Griquas jersey (navy blue), Kimberley
3rd test – Villagers club (white), Cape Town
1896
1st test – Crusader (white), Port Elizabeth
2nd test – Griquas (navy blue), Kimberley
3rd test – Transvaal jersey (white with red), Johannesburg
4th test – Old Diocesans College (olive green), Cape Town
1903
1st test – plain white jersey, Johannesburg
2nd test – Griquas (navy blue), Kimberley
3rd test – plain green jersey, Cape Town
1906–07 tour – dark green jersey with white collars
These colours were repeated against Ireland in Dublin in 2006 to celebrate the centenary of the Springboks' first overseas tour.

— SPRINGBOKS NOT SO GREEN —

Since 1906 the Springboks have played only eleven test matches in jerseys coloured other than their traditional green, and in each instance it was in a basically white shirt.

24 Nov 1906 v Ireland in Belfast – white shirts
30 Nov 1912 v Ireland in Dublin – white shirts

In December 1931 South Africa once more visited Dublin, but this time the Irishmen graciously allowed the Springboks to wear their traditional green jerseys.

Australia's original colours also included green shirts – it was not until 1961 that they adopted the gold shirts we see today. Accordingly, for the Wallabies' 1953 visit to South Africa, the Springboks donned white jerseys for the two tests. By the time of South Africa's next game against Ireland the convention had altered to the home side changing in the event of a colour clash.

Here is a list of all instances since 1906 where South Africa took to the field in a test match not wearing green shirts:

1953 v Australia (all four tests) – White shirts/black shorts
13 May 1961 – v Ireland (Cape Town) – White shirts/black shorts
1981 v Ireland (both tests) – White shirts/black shorts
1998 v Ireland (both tests) – White shirts with green shoulders/black shorts/black socks
2004 v Ireland (both tests) – White shirts /white shorts/green and gold socks
2010 v Ireland (Dublin) – White shirts /white shorts/green and gold socks

— SAME SCORE —

There were four occasions in Springbok history when two consecutive tests ended with the same score.

8–3	against Wales and Ireland in 1931
25–3	against France in 1952 and Australia in 1953
9–0	against Australia in 1956 (first and second tests)
22–16	against Australia and New Zealand in 2005

Amazingly the Springboks of 1906, 1931 and 1951 all defeated Oxford University by 24 points to 3 at the Iffley Road ground in Oxford.

The Springboks of 1912 and 1931 beat their opponents 8–3 at the Gnoll ground in Neath, playing against Neath in 1912 and a combined Neath & Aberavon side in 1931.

— HAPPY HOOKERS —

The **Cockrell** brothers Charlie (1969–70) and Robert (1974–81) played hooker for South Africa and Western Province. A third brother, William, also played hooker for Western Province, and Robert's son Robin played hooker for Western Province and Griqualand West.

The **Wessels** brothers Piet (1951–52) and John (1965) played hooker for South Africa and Free State. Piet played for Transvaal later in his career. A third brother, Koos, was a Junior Springbok hooker in 1955.

— BASTARD! —

In 1937 when Ebbo Bastard, the Natal flank, was chosen for the Springbok side to Australia and New Zealand, they received a telegram: 'Best of luck. You are the most representative side ever to have left our shores: Sixteen Afrikaners, ten Englishmen, one Jew and a Bastard!'

— TONDERAI'S RECORD-BREAKING START —

On 11 June 2005 Tonderai Chavhanga, the Zimbabwean-born winger, wrote his name into the record books by scoring six tries on his Springbok debut in the record-breaking win over Uruguay at the Absa Stadium (previously known as the Basil Kenyon Stadium) in East London. Chavhanga, who coincidentally was also the youngest player in the team, was dropped for the Springboks' next test match against France and had to wait for two years before appearing in his second test, against New Zealand as a replacement for Jaco Pretorius on 14 July 2007 at the Jade Stadium in Christchurch.

Before Tonderai Chavhanga scored his six tries against Uruguay, Stefan Terblanche was the record-holder for most test tries on debut when he scored four against Ireland on 13 June 1998 at the Free State Stadium in Bloemfontein.

— TRY, TRY, TRY AGAIN —

The former Lions and Cats centre Jaque Fourie made a barnstorming start to his Springbok career, uniquely crossing for tries on each of his first three appearances during the 2003 Rugby World Cup in Australia. Jacque's magic start began with a try in the 35th minute of his debut against Uruguay in Perth and then followed with another against Georgia at the Sydney Football Stadium. He was a bench replacement against Samoa in Brisbane but came on for the last nine minutes, still finding enough time to score again and set his personal milestone. In 2010 Willem Alberts, coincidentally from the same school as Fourie – Monument High School in Krugersdorp – also scored tries in his first three test. What makes Alberts' tries more remarkable is the fact that he came on as a substitute in all three tests. He scored his first try against Wales in the 51th minute, only four minutes after making his debut. He also scored tries against Scotland and England.

— FASTEST TRIES —

15s Fourie du Preez, v New Zealand at Wellington on 22 July 2006.
17s Breyton Paulse, v France at Johannesburg on 16 June 2001.
23s Jean de Villiers, v New Zealand at Christchurch on 24 July 2004.
1st minute – André Snyman v France in Paris on 22 November 1997.
1st minute – Ruben Kruger v New Zealand in Auckland on 9 August 1997.
64s Joost van der Westhuizen v Uruguay at Perth on 11 Oct 2003.
Note: Jacque Fourie scored a try within a minute of coming on as a replacement against Samoa at Brisbane during the World Cup on 1 November 2003.

— FASTEST DEBUT TRY —

Stefan Terblanche scored within 4 minutes of his debut against Ireland in Bloemfontein on 13 June 1998.

Willem Alberts scored within 4 minutes of his debut against Wales in Cardiff on 13 November 2010.

Delarey du Preez scored within two minutes of coming on as a replacement on his Springbok debut against Samoa in Pretoria on 6 July 2002.

Bryan Habana scored within a minute of coming on as a replacement with his first touch on his debut against England at Twickenham on 20 November 2004.

— TRIES IN MOST SUCCESSIVE GAMES —

Danie Gerber scored tries in six successive Springbok appearances between 1982 and 1984, including two try hat-tricks; against South America in Pretoria and England at Johannesburg.

The feat was equalled by Chester Williams from the first test against Argentina in Port Elizabeth in October 1994 until the World Cup quarter-final match against Samoa in Johannesburg the following June.

Tests	Name	Started	Ended
6	Danie Gerber	v S. America (27 Mar 1982)	v Cavaliers (10 May 1986)
6	Chester Williams	v Argentina (8 Oct 1994)	v France (17 Jun 1995)
5	Pieter Rossouw	v NZ (9 Aug 1997)	v England (29 Jul 1997)
4	Joel Stransky	v Argentina (8 Oct 1994)	v Romania (30 May 1995)
4	Joost van der Westhuizen	v Ireland (20 Jun 1998)	v New Zealand (25 Jul 1998)
4	Jean de Villiers	v Pacific Is (17 Jul 2004)	v Australia (21 Aug 2004)
4	Bryan Habana	v England (26 May 2007)	v England (14 Sep 2007)
4	Juan Smith	v England (14 Sep 2007)	v Argentina (14 Oct 2007)

— ONE ALL TOO BRIEF CAP —

Schutte Bekker, the Northern Transvaal loose forward, replaced Gary Teichmann for a blood bin for only two minutes against Australia at Loftus Versfeld in Pretoria on 23 August 1997 to win his only test cap. His is the shortest-ever Springbok test career in terms of playing time.

Leon Vogel, the Free State wing, replaced Dawie Snyman, who previously went on for Ian McCallum in the 69th minute, against the British Lions in the second test at Loftus Versfeld in Pretoria in 1974 for the last five minutes of the game. Coincidentally Vogel was a late replacement on the bench for Gerrie Germishuys when Germishuys took the place of the injured Gert Muller in the test side.

Dan van Zyl was another who gained just five minutes playing time in tests, although he did sit on the bench for another eight complete games. Van Zyl's only cap came against England at Twickenham in 2000 as a 75th minute replacement for scrumhalf Joost van der Westhuizen.

— SPRINGBOK DEMOS —

When Dawie de Villiers took his Springbok team to the United Kingdom and Ireland in 1969–70 there were anti-apartheid demonstrations almost everywhere they went. Among the most vociferous was at Swansea on 15 November 1969 at their fourth game. Some of the most amazing scenes in the history of Springbok rugby occurred at St Helens when about 40 demonstrators burst onto the field and staged a sit-down protest shortly after half-time. There had been tension outside the ground before the game started, but when the demonstrators invaded the pitch they received short shrift. The police, joined by Swansea RFC 'stewards', cleared the spectators within five minutes to allow the game to continue.

The police conducted an investigation into the handling of the pitch invasion and exonerated their officers and the 'stewards', but from then on the police dealt with all operations at matches.

When the Springboks played Wales at the Arms Park, the pitch was ringed with barbed wire to ensure nobody got onto the pitch.

One of the leaders of the demonstrations was Peter Hain, who went on to become Secretary of State for Wales and Member of Parliament for Neath.

On the Springbok tour to New Zealand in 1981 things got even worse. The second match of the tour was to be against Waikato in Hamilton. Pat McQuarrie, an old fighter pilot, stole a light airoplane in Taupo and threatened to fly Into the main pavillion if the game went on. The game was cancelled. On the Friday night before the first test in Christchurch the team stayed at the squash courts of the Linwood club; in Wellington and in Auckland the team stayed in the pavilions of the test venues – not ideal preparation for any match. The third and last test at Eden Park is still known as the 'Flour bomb' test. A light aircraft circled around the field for the duration of the game, dropping flour bombs onto the field. One of these flour bombs hit the New Zealand prop Gary Knight on the head and he had to receive medical treatment.

— HAT-TRICKS GALORE —

Ray Mordt scored three tries in the third and final test match against New Zealand at Eden Park in 1981. In the Springboks' next test match, against the United States Eagles, he scored three tries again, the only Springbok to achieve this feat in consecutive tests. The first hat-trick for the Springboks was by 'Boetie' McHardy, the Free State wing, against Ireland at Lansdowne Road, Dublin on 30 November 1912. The other wing, Jan Stegmann, also scored a hat-trick in the same match. This feat was only repeated 95 years later when the two flanks, Juan Smith and Schalk Burger, both scored hat-tricks against Namibia on 15 August 2007 at Newlands in Cape Town. Apart from Ray Mordt, the following Springboks have scored two hat-tricks in their career: Danie Gerber (against South America at Loftus Versfeld in Pretoria in 1982 and against England at Ellis Park in Johannesburg in 1984); Joost van der Westhuizen (against Wales at Cardiff Arms Park in 1996 and against Uruguay in Perth in 2003 at the RWC). Stefan Terblanche never scored exactly three tries in a test; he scored four tries on debut against Ireland at the Free State Stadium in Bloemfontein in 1998 and five tries against Italy at King's Park in Durban in 1999.

Joost van der Westhuizen is the only Springbok captain to score a hat-trick – against Uruguay in the 2003 RWC.

No opposing player has ever scored a hat-trick of tries against South Africa in a test match.

— FASTEST TRY HAT-TRICKS —

The fastest Springbok test try hat-trick was scored in just seven minutes by Pieter Rossouw during their record 96–13 demolition of Wales at Loftus Versfeld in June 1998. Rossouw scored his first try (and South Africa's 5th) on the stroke of half-time and then followed this up with tries in the 42nd and 46th minutes.

Time	Name	Opponents (Venue)	Date
7 mins	Pieter Rossouw	Wales (Pretoria)	27 Jun 1998
12 mins	Tom van Vollenhoven	British Isles (Cape Town)	20 Aug 1955
17 mins	Danie Gerber	England (Johannesburg)	9 Jun 1984*

Time	Name	Opponents (Venue)	Date
c20 mins	Boetie McHardy	Ireland (Dublin)	30 Nov 1912*
20 mins	Deon Kayser	Italy (Durban)	19 Jun 1999
23 mins	Jongi Nokwe	Australia (Johannesburg)	30 Aug 2008
29 mins	Ray Mordt	New Zealand (Auckland)	12 Sep 1981#

Notes: Tonderai Chavhanga scored his 4th, 5th and 6th tries against Uruguay in East London on 11 June 2005 in a spell of just 15 minutes, and managed to tally four tries in the second half alone. Stefan Terblanche scored three tries in 16 minutes against Italy in Durban on 19 Jun 1999, but these were his 2nd, 3rd and 4th tries of the match. Pieter Rossouw scored three tries in 20 minutes against France in Paris on 22 Nov 1997, but these were his 2nd, 3rd and 4th tries of the game. Bryan Habana scored three tries in 20 minutes (all in the second half) against Samoa in Paris on 9 September 2003, but these were his 2nd, 3rd and 4th tries of the game. Deon Kayser achieved his as a replacement.
* three in 1st half
# three in 2nd half

— FASTEST HAT-TRICK FROM THE START OF A TEST —

Danie Gerber scored the fastest hat-trick from the start of a game after scoring his third try against England in 1984 after just 32 minutes.

Time	Name	Opponents (Venue)	Date
32 mins	Danie Gerber	England (Johannesburg)	9 Jun 1984*
36 mins	Jongi Nokwe	Australia (Johannesburg)	30 Aug 2008

Note: Deon Kayser recorded a hat-trick within 23 minutes of coming on as a replacement against Italy in Durban on 19 June 1999.

— A CENTURY FOR DANEEL —

George Daneel is the only test-playing Springbok to have reached a 100th birthday. George Murray Daneel was born in Calvinia in the Northern Cape on 29 August 1904. The back-rower attended Robertson Boys High School, University of Cape Town and Stellenbosch University and was playing for Western Province when he made the first of 8 test appearances for the Springboks between 1928 and 1932. He went on to become a Dutch Reformed Church minister and was chief chaplain to the South African forces during the Second World War. When he was 98 George was asked about his health and replied: 'My health is first class. Just my knees give me a bit of trouble. I can't jog or play tennis any more!'

George died peacefully on 19 October 2004 at his daughter's home in Franschhoek in the Western Cape.

— OLDEST EVER SPRINGBOKS —

Age	Name	Born	Died	Caps
100y 51d	George Daneel	29 Aug 1904	19 Oct 2004	8
97y 228d	JC van der Westhuizen	22 Nov 1905	8 Jul 2003	4
97y 169d	Jan Stegmann	21 Jun 1887	7 Dec 1984	5
97y 67d	Frank Douglass	15 Jul 1875	20 Sep 1972	1
96y 237d	Bertram van der Plank	29 Apr 1894	22 Dec 1990	2
94y 251d	Danie Theunissen	12 Jul 1869	19 Mar 1964	1
94y 170d	Howard Watt	1 March 1911	18 Aug 2005	0
92y 363d	Ginger Clark	22 Sep 1906	20 Sep 1999	1
91y 232d	DC 'Mary' Jackson	21 Apr 1885	9 Dec 1976	3
91y 78d	Frankie Waring	7 Nov 1908	24 Jan 2000	7

— BOKS' MAGIC RUN —

The Springboks enjoyed a run of seventeen straight test wins under coaches Carel du Plessis and Nick Mallett between their victory over the Wallabies at Loftus Versfeld in August 1997 until the loss to England (7–13) at Twickenham on 5 December 1998.

The sequence began with Du Plessis' last game in charge.

Top seventeen

Win	Date	Opponents	Venue	Result
1	23 Aug 1997	Australia	Pretoria	Won 61–22
2	8 Nov 1997	Italy	Bologna	Won 62–31

Win	Date	Opponents	Venue	Result
3	15 Nov 1997	France (1st test)	Lyon	Won 36–32
4	22 Nov 1997	France (2nd test)	Paris	Won 52–10
5	29 Nov 1997	England	Twickenham	Won 29–11
6	6 Dec 1997	Scotland	Murrayfield	Won 68–10
7	13 Jun 1998	Ireland (1st test)	Bloemfontein	Won 37–13
8	20 Jun 1998	Ireland (2nd test)	Pretoria	Won 33–0
9	27 Jun 1998	Wales	Pretoria	Won 96–13
10	4 Jul 1998	England	Cape Town	Won 18–0
11	18 Jul 1998	Australia	Perth	Won 14–13
12	25 Jul 1998	New Zealand	Wellington	Won 13–3
13	15 Aug 1998	New Zealand	Durban	Won 24–23
14	22 Aug 1998	Australia	Johannesburg	Won 29–15
15	14 Nov 1998	Wales	Wembley	Won 28–20
16	21 Nov 1998	Scotland	Murrayfield	Won 35–10
17	28 Nov 1998	Ireland	Dublin	Won 27–13

— NIGHTMARE SEVEN —

The Springboks' worst losing run is seven games, beginning with the loss to France in Springs in July 1964 and ending with their 19–16 victory over New Zealand in the 3rd test at Christchurch on 4 September 1965.

Loss	Date	Opponents	Venue	Result
1	25 Jul 1964	France	Springs	Lost 6–8
2	10 Apr 1965	Ireland	Dublin	Lost 6–9
3	17 Apr 1965	Scotland	Murrayfield	Lost 5–8
4	19 Jun 1965	Australia (1st test)	Sydney	Lost 11–18
5	26 Jun 1965	Australia (2nd test)	Brisbane	Lost 8–12
6	31 Jul 1965	New Zealand (1st test)	Wellington	Lost 3–6
7	21 Aug 1965	New Zealand (2nd test)	Dunedin	Lost 0–13

— TRAGEDY OF TWO YOUNG STARS —

David Gill (Davie) Cope has the honour of being the first Springbok to have scored points with the boot in a test match when he converted Theo Samuel's second try in the 2nd test against Great Britain at the Old Wanderers ground in Johannesburg on 22 August 1896 on his one and only test appearance. Davie, at the age of 19 years 8 days, remains to this day the youngest player to have scored points for South Africa. However, tragedy cut short the Transvaal fullback's young life. Just two days after his 21st birthday he was travelling with another Transvaal player, AM Tait, for a Currie Cup match in Cape Town when a railway accident at the treacherous Mostert's Hoek pass near Matjiesfontein in the Western Cape claimed the lives of both young men.

Amazingly Theo Samuels, South Africa's first try-scorer, remains the second-youngest Springbok to die when typhoid ended his young life aged 23 in Johannesburg in 1896 only two months after his third and final test appearance.

— FREE STATE WINGS —

The two wings chosen for the first test against the All Blacks in Durban in 1976 were Gerrie Germishuys and Edrich Krantz, both from the Free State and the University of the Orange Free State. One of the reserves was Hermanus Potgieter, another Free State wing who also played his club rugby for the University of the Orange Free State (Shimlas). Unfortunately Potgieter had to withdraw following a hamstring injury suffered for the Gazelles against the All Blacks on the Tuesday before the test. He was replaced on the bench by Joggie Jansen, himself an old Shimlas (UOFS) player. The two wings scored the only two tries in the match, with Gerrie Germishuys scoring South Africa's 300th test try and Edrich Krantz grabbing a try on debut.

— PROVINCIAL CRICKETERS —

All three flyhalves on the 1956 tour to Australia and New Zealand were provincial cricketers: Clive Ulyate for Eastern Province and Transvaal, Brian Pfaff for Western Province and PeeWee Howe for Border.

Other Springboks who also played provincial cricket were: Chubb Vigne (Griqualand West), Tiny Francis (Free State), Dirk Jackson (Transvaal and WP), Sarel Strauss (Griqualand West), Howard Watt

(WP), Norman Riley (Free State), Morné du Plessis (WP), Barry Wolmarans (Free State), Helgard Müller (Free State).

Nick Mallett was an Oxford University double blue for cricket and rugby.

The Newlands tests of 1891, 1896 and 1903 were all refereed by double Springboks (for cricket and rugby) – HH Castens, Alf Richards and Biddy Anderson.

— ENGLISH UNIVERSITY BLUES —

The first Springbok captain, HH Castens, was also the first English university Blue to play for South Africa. The most recent one was Andrew Aitken. Here is the complete list:

Name	University	Blues	Caps	Years
HH Castens	Oxford	1886–87	1 cap	1891
Noel Howe-Browne	Oxford	1905–06	3 caps	1910
Fanie Cronjé	Oxford	1907–08	0 caps	1912
Dirkie de Villiers	Cambridge	1913	3 caps	1910
Willie Rousseau	Oxford	1929	2 caps	1928
Stanley Osler	Oxford	1931	1 cap	1928
Paul Johnstone	Oxford	1952–54	9 caps	1951–56
Tommy Bedford	Oxford	1965–67	25 caps	1963–71
Dugald Macdonald	Oxford	1975–76	1 cap	1974
John Robbie	Cambridge	1977–78	0 caps	1984
Nick Mallett	Oxford	1979	2 caps	1984
Andrew Aitken	Oxford	1993	7 caps	1997–98

— FOUR FIRST NAMES —

Four Springbok internationals have had four first names:
Pieter Albertus Ryno Otto NEL
Noel Richard Frank George HOWE-BROWN
Willem Ferdinand van Rheede van Oudtshoorn BERGH
Arthur Frederick William Douglas MARSBERG

— TEENAGE BOKS —

To Jack Hartley belongs the honour of being the youngest player on debut. He was just 18 years and 18 days old in 1891 when he played against the touring team from Great Britain. The list of players who were younger than 20 years of age on debut is:

Age	Name	Born	Position	Match
18y 18d	Jack Hartley	18 Aug 1873	Wing	v GB (5 Sep 1891)
19y 8d	Davie Cope	14 Aug 1877	Fullback	v GB (22 Aug 1896)
19y 37d	Bob Loubser	6 Aug 1884	Wing	v GB (12 Sep 1903)
19y 51d	Clive van Ryneveld	7 Jul 1891	Halfback	v GB (27 Aug 1910)
19y 72d	Wally Mills	16 Jun 1891	Wing	v GB (27 Aug 1910)
19y 112d	Freddy Turner	18 Mar 1914	Wing	v Australia (8 Jul 1933)
19y 126d	'Fairy' Heatlie	25 Apr 1872	Forward	v GB (29 Aug 1891)
19y 158d	Syd de Melker	31 Mar 1884	Centre	v GB (5 Sep 1903)
19y 181d	François Steyn	14 May 1987	Wing	v Ireland (11 Nov 2006)
19y 230d	Steve Joubert	8 Apr 1887	Fullback	v Ireland (24 Nov 1906)
19y 260d	Jackie Powell	12 Dec 1871	Halfback	v GB (29 Aug 1891)
19y 321d	Percy Jones	13 Sep 1876	Wing	v GB (30 Jul 1896)
19y 349d	Chilliboy Ralepelle	11 Sep 1986	rep	v NZ (26 Aug 2006)

Both Wally Mills and François Steyn scored tries, therefore Mills is the youngest-ever Springbok try-scorer. Davie Cope kicked a conversion and is the youngest points-scorer.

François Steyn became the youngest player to drop a goal on the occasion of his 2nd cap against England at Twickenham on 18 November 2006 aged 19 years and 188 days.

South Africa's youngest captain was Avril Malan against New Zealand in Bloemfontein on 13 August 1960 on his 3rd test appearance aged just 23 years and 126 days.

— 35-YEAR-OLDS —

Johan Ackermann is the oldest player in his last appearance to have represented South Africa at 37 years and 34 days. The complete list of players older than 35 years of age on their last appearance is:

Age	Name	Born	Position	Match	Caps
37y 34d	Johan Ackermann	3 Jun 1970	Lock	v Australia (7 Jul 2007)	13
36y 258d	Boy Morkel	2 Jan 1885	Eightman	v NZ (17 Sep 1921)	9
35y 277d	Deon Lötter	10 Nov 1957	Flank	v Australia (14 Aug 1993)	3
35y 252d	Frik du Preez	28 Nov 1935	Lock	v Australia (7 Aug 1971)	38
35y 208d	Flip Geel	7 Feb 1914	Lock	v NZ (3 Sep 1949)	1
35y 130d	Louis Moolman	21 Jan 1951	Lock	v Cavaliers (31 May 1986)	24
35y 100d	Flip Nel	17 Jun 1902	Lock	v NZ (25 Sep 1937)	16
35y 42d*	Willie Kahts	20 Feb 1947	Hooker	v S. America (3 Apr 1982)	10
35y 42d	Os du Randt	8 Sep 1972	Prop	v England (20 Oct 2007)	79
35y 32d	Lofty Nel	11 Aug 1935	Eightman	v NZ (12 Sep 1970)	11
35y 3d	Willie Meyer	6 Nov 1967	Prop	v England (9 Nov 2002)	26

*Kahts lived for one more leap year than Du Randt and therefore is ranked as older!

Boy Morkel and Flip Nel were captains in their last tests.

Flip Geel was making his one and only Springbok appearance, but the oldest Springbok on debut is Deon Lötter on 3 July 1993 against France in Johannesburg aged 36 years 235 days.

The oldest try-scorer is Os du Randt who crossed against Namibia in Cape Town on 15 August 2007 aged 34 years and 341 days in his 73rd test appearance.

The oldest to kick points was Naas Botha against England at Twickenham on 14 November 1992 with a conversion, a dropped goal and two penalty goals when aged 34 years 261 days, in his 28th test appearance.

— BIRTHDAY BOYS —

Quite a few players have represented the Springboks on their birthdays. Kevin de Klerk and Theuns Stofberg both celebrated their birthday playing against Ireland on 6 June 1981, and André Venter and JP Pietersen scored tries on their birthdays. Tommy Laubscher made his debut on his 31st birthday in 1994.

The list of players who represented South Africa on their birthdays are:

Age	Name	Date	Cap	Position	Opponent	Notes
26	Bob Loubser	6 Aug 1910	6	Wing	v GB	
27	Bertus van der Merwe	14 Jul 1956	6	Hooker	v NZ	
26	Keith Oxlee	17 Dec 1960	6	Flyhalf	v Ireland	
24	John Gainsford	4 Aug 1962	15	Centre	v Lions	
27	Stompie van der Merwe	24 Aug 1963	3	Lock	v Australia	
27	Gert Kotze	12 Aug 1967	4	Prop	v France	
29	Charlie Cockrell	10 Jan 1970	2	Hooker	v Ireland	
29	Kevin de Klerk	6 Jun 1981	13	Lock	v Ireland	
26	Theuns Stofberg	6 Jun 1981	14	Flank	v Ireland	
29	Hennie Bekker	12 Sep 1981	2	Lock	v NZ	
31	Tommy Laubscher	8 Oct 1994	1	Prop	v Argentina	

Age	Name	Date	Cap	Position	Opponent	Notes
28	André Venter	14 Nov 1998	29	Flank	v Wales	Try
24	Robbie Fleck	17 Jul 1999	4	Centre	v Australia	
22	De Wet Barry	24 Jun 2000	3	Centre	v England	
29	Quinton Davids	17 Jul 2004	8	rep	v Pacific Islands	
24	Juan Smith	30 Jul 2005	15	Flank	v Australia	
25	CJ van der Linde	27 Aug 2005	21	Prop	v NZ	
28	De Wet Barry	24 Jun 2006	39	Centre	v France	
28	Bakkies Botha	22 Sep 2007	40	Lock	v Tonga	
22	JP Pietersen	12 Jul 2008	17	Wing	v NZ	Try
29	Gurthrö Steenkamp	12 Jun 2010	23	Prop	v France	Try
27	Bryan Habana	12 Jun 2010	58	Wing	V France	

— THE 750-CAP TEAM —

The most experienced Springbok team of all time was the one which took the field in the Tri-Nations match at Bloemfontein against Australia on 4 September 2010. The starting lineup, boasting the staggering total of 750 test caps between them, was as follows:

No	Name	Caps
15	François Steyn	38
14	JP Pietersen	35
13	Jaque Fourie	61

No	Name	Caps
12	Jean de Villiers	62
11	Bryan Habana	65
10	Morné Steyn	20
9	Francois Hougaard	4
8	Pierre Spies	38
7	Juan Smith	64
6	Schalk Burger	62
5	Victor Matfield	100
4	Danie Rossouw	53
3	Jannie du Plessis	19
2	John Smit (capt)	101
1	Guthrö Steenkamp	30

— FLUSH OF YOUTH —

The youngest team was selected for South Africa's second ever test match against Great Britain at Kimberley on 29 August 1891. The average age was just 23 years 135 days.

Position	Name	Caps	Age
Fullback	Ben Duff	2	23
Wing	Harry Boyes	2	23
Centre	Chubb Vigne	2	22
Centre	Arthur de Kock	1	25
Flyhalf	Alf Richards	2	23
Scrumhalf	Jackie Powell	1	19
Forwards	Oupa Versfeld	2	31
	Bob Snedden (capt)	1	24
	Bob Shand	1	25
	Wilfred Trenery	1	23
	Japie Louw	2	23
	Dan Smith	1	22

Position	Name	Caps	Age
	Frederick Alexander	2	20
	Barry Heatlie	1	19
	Toski Smith	1	20

— EXPERIENCE IS KEY —

The oldest team to represent the Springboks was against the World XV at Cape Town on 26 August 1989, with an average age of 29 years and 82 days.

No	Name	Caps	Age
15	Johan Heunis	13	31
14	Kobus Burger	1	25
13	Faffa Knoetze	1	26
12	Michael du Plessis	7	30
11	Carel du Plessis	11	29
10	Naas Botha	22	31
9	Garth Wright	3	25
8	Jannie Breedt (capt)	5	30
7	Gert Smal	5	27
6	Burger Geldenhuys	6	33
5	Adolf Malan	1	27
4	Niel Hugo	1	30
3	Flippie van der Merwe	6	32
2	Uli Schmidt	5	28
1	Heinrich Rodgers	1	27

— THE YOUNG MEN —

The honour of being the youngest member of the starting lineup the most times is Bryan Habana with 17.

No	Name	Position(s)	Years
17	Bryan Habana	Wing	2004–07
15	JP Pietersen	Fullback/Wing	2006*–08
14	Os du Randt	Prop	1994*–96
15	François Steyn	Centre/Fullback/Flyhalf	2007*–09
12	Schalk Burger, jr	Flank	2004–06

* From debut

— THE SENIOR CITIZENS —

Being the oldest player on duty in the starting lineup fell on Os du Randt on an incredible 36 occasions.

No	Name	Position	Years
36	Os du Randt	Prop	2004–07
19	Frik du Preez	Lock	1967–71
17	Willie Meyer	Prop	1999–2002
16	André Joubert	Fullback	1995–97
13	Johan Claassen	Lock	1960–62
13	Victor Matfield	Lock	2008–09
11	Willie Kahts	Hooker	1980–82
11	Henry Honiball	Centre/ Flyhalf	1997–99

— LEAST EXPERIENCED BENCH —

Uniquely, all six players on the bench against the British Lions in the first test match on 8 June 1974 in Cape Town had NO test experience between them.
They were:
Gerrie Germishuys

Gerald Bosch
Paul Bayvel
Rampie Stander
André Bestbier
Dugald Macdonald

— MOST EXPERIENCED BENCH —

This was at the World Cup pool game against Tonga in Lens, France on 22 September 2007. This was the only occasion that the Springbok bench has tallied over 300 caps. The actual tally before kick-off was an amazing 311 caps.

No	Name	Caps
16	John Smit	69
17	BJ Botha	14
18	Victor Matfield	62
19	Juan Smith	36
20	Bryan Habana	30
21	François Steyn	11
22	Percy Montgomery	89

— POINTS IN MOST SUCCESSIVE APPEARANCES —

Naas Botha is the only Springbok to have scored points in all 28 tests he played in. Percy Montgomery scored points in 26 consecutive tests he played in between 2004 and 2006.

The list is:

Tests	Names	Started/Ended	
28	Naas Botha	v S. America (26 Apr 1980)	Entire career
26	Percy Montgomery	v Ireland (19 Jun 2004)	v Australia (15 Jul 2006)
24	Morné Steyn	v B & I Lions (27 June 2009)	Last 24 test appearances
18	Braam van Straaten	v Australia (17 Jul 1999)	Last 18 test appearances

Tests	Names	Started/Ended	
18	Percy Montgomery	v NZ (22 Jul 2006)	v Wales (14 Jun 2008)
15	Piet Visagie	v France (29 Jul 1967)	v NZ (8 Aug 1970)
11	Louis Koen	v USA (1 Dec 2001)	v NZ (8 Nov 2003)

— TRYLESS SPELLS —

The only Springbok to gain over 50 caps without scoring a try is Victor Matfield, whose sixth test try came in the 28th minute of South Africa's test against Australia in Cape Town on 8 August 2009. Subsequently Matfield has gained 56 caps and played for 4 335 minutes on the pitch without crossing the whitewash.

Tests	Name	From	To	Details
56	Victor Matfield	21 Aug 2004	8 Aug 2009	
47	Os du Randt	8 Nov 1997	15 Aug 2007	
36	John Smit	26 Jun 2004	9 Jun 2007	
33	Hannes Marais	23 May 1964	30 Nov 1974#	Last 33 tests
33	Ollie le Roux	3 Oct 1999	17 Aug 2002#	Last 33 tests
32	CJ van der Linde	16 Nov 2002*	25 Nov 2006	First 32 tests
29	Cobus Visagie	12 Jun 1999*	28 Jun 2003#	entire career
27	Lionel Wilson	13 Aug 1960*	18 Sep 1965#	entire career
27	De Wet Barry	6 Jul 2002	24 Jun 2006#	Last 27 tests
25	AJ Venter	26 Nov 2000*	9 Sep 2006#	entire career
25	Albert van den Berg	11 Jun 2005	24 Nov 2007#	Last 25 tests

* Test debut

Last test appearance

— SUPER RUGBY DEBUT AFTER SPRINGBOK DEBUT —

Since the advent of the Super 12 competition in 1996, 22 players have made their test debut for the Springboks before making their bow in Super Rugby.

Name	SA Debut	Super Rugby debut
Dawie Theron	3 Aug 1996 (v Australia)	28 Feb 1998 (Cats v Bulls)
Henry Tromp	17 Aug 1996 (v NZ)	1 Mar 1997 (Lions v Blues)
André Venter	17 Aug 1996 (v NZ)	2 Mar 1997 (Free State v Lions)
Russell Bennett	10 Jun 1997 (v Tonga)	20 Mar 1998 (Sharks v Highlanders)
Andrew Aitken	22 Nov 1997 (v France)	27 Feb 1998 (Stormers v Hurricanes)
Franco Smith	6 Dec 1997 (v Scotland)	28 Feb 1998 (Bulls v Cats)
Gaffie du Toit	13 Jun 1998 (v Ireland)	8 May 1999 (Cats v Reds)
Kaya Malotana	10 Oct 1999 (v Spain)	20 Apr 2002 (Cats v Reds)
Marius Joubert	21 Jul 2001 (v NZ)	22 Feb 2002 (Stormers v Sharks)
Joe van Niekerk	21 Jul 2001 (v NZ)	26 Apr 2002 (Cats v Crusaders)
Lawrence Sephaka	1 Dec 2001 (v USA)	23 Feb 2002 (Cats v Bulls)
Brent Russell	8 Jun 2002 (v Wales)	21 Feb 2003 (Sharks v Stormers)
Jean de Villiers	9 Nov 2002 (v France)	25 Feb 2005 (Stormers v Sharks)
CJ van der Linde	16 Nov 2002 (v Scotland)	27 Feb 2004 (Cats v Brumbies)
Schalk Burger	24 Oct 2003 (v Georgia)	13 Mar 2004 (Stormers v Waratahs)
Tim Dlulane	6 Nov 2004 (v Wales)	11 Mar 2006 (Bulls v Highlanders)
Michael Claassens	6 Nov 2004 (v Wales)	26 Feb 2005 (Cats v Bulls)
Bryan Habana	20 Nov 2004 (v England)	26 Feb 2005 (Bulls v Cats)
Meyer Bosman	19 Nov 2005 (v Wales)	10 Feb 2006 (Cheetahs v Bulls)

Name	SA Debut	Super Rugby debut
Jaco Pretorius	11 Nov 2006 (v Ireland)	10 Feb 2007 (Lions v Highlanders)
François Steyn	11 Nov 2006 (v Ireland)	3 Feb 2007 (Sharks v Bulls)
Hilton Lobberts	19 Nov 2006 (v England)	3 Feb 2007 (Bulls v Sharks)
Elton Jantjies	4 Dec 2010 (v Barbarians)	19 Feb 20111 (Lions vs Bulls)

Of these, four had to wait more than a year to make their Super rugby debut: Kaya Malotana (923 days), Jean de Villiers (839 days), Dawie Theron (574 days), and CJ van der Linde (468 days).

— A CENTURY OF POINTS IN A CALENDAR YEAR —

Percy Montgomery leads the way for total test points scored in a calendar year – his 219 points in 2007 was a world record.

Year	Name	Points	Tests	T	Conv	Pens	DG
1995	Joel Stransky	112	8+1	2	12	23	3
1998	Percy Montgomery	111	12	2	25	17	–
1999	Jannie de Beer	102	6	–	18	16	6
2000	Braam van Straaten	136	9+2	2	12	34	–
2002	André Pretorius	102	9+1	2	22	15	1
2003	Louis Koen	120	9+2	–	15	28	2
2004*	Percy Montgomery	154	11	1	28	31	–
2005*	Percy Montgomery	158	12	1	24	32	3
2007*	Percy Montgomery	219	12+2	5	52	30	–
2009	Morné Steyn	137	9+3	1	12	31	5
2010	Morné Steyn	185	13	3	25	40	–

* World record that particular year.

Only four other South Africans have scored more points than any other player in the world in a calendar year of test rugby:

1933	Gerry Brand	17	5	–	2	3	1
1949	Okey Geffin	32	4	–	1	10	–
1953	Natie Rens	19	2	–	5	2	1
1980	Naas Botha	86	9	–	19	10	6

— GOALS FROM A MARK —

In the period from 1928 to 1937 only Bennie Osler and Gerry Brand kicked points for the Springboks by way of conversions, penalty goals or dropped goals, but sandwiched in between is a peculiar three points. In the second test against the 1928 All Blacks at Ellis Park, skipper Phil Mostert caught a 'mark', and to the surprise of everyone this massive forward scored three points with a 45-yard drop kick. No one could ever recall having seen Mostert put over a dropped kick in a match before.

The only goal from a mark scored against South Africa was kicked by British fullback Willie Mitchell at Kimberley on 29 August 1891. It was the only scoring action in a 3–nil win for the visitors.

This method of scoring ceased when the free kick clause was introduced in 1978.

— PERCENTAGE OF SPRINGBOK POINTS SCORED DURING A TEST CAREER —

Braam van Straaten scored the highest percentage of Springbok points during his test career. Morné Steyn is in second place. The list is:

%	Player	Player points	Springbok points*
56,52%	Braam van Straaten	221	391
52.52%	Morné Steyn	322	613
50,73%	Naas Botha	312	615
47,01%	Jannie de Beer	181	385
45,71%	Joel Stransky	240	525
38,14%	Louis Koen	135	354
34,39%	Piet Visagie	130	378
30,44%	Percy Montgomery	893	2 933

* Points South Africa scored whilst player actually on the pitch.

— NELSON MANDELA CHALLENGE PLATE —

The Nelson Mandela Challenge Plate was first contested in 2000. The original concept involved a one-off match (outside the Tri-Nations Series) to be contested every two years, alternating between Australia and South Africa.

The inaugural Nelson Mandela Challenge Plate match was played at Melbourne's Telstra Dome on 8 July 2000, with the Wallabies winning the contest 44–23. Prior to the match, Mr Mandela addressed the crowd and television audience via satellite. John Eales raised the Plate, which is a sleek, silver plate of classic design with a thick 24-carat rim and a central gold disk featuring a Wallaby and a Springbok. To emphasise the link with rugby, the back of the Plate is leather-clad.

It literally is a plate, hence the name Nelson Mandela Challenge Plate as opposed to Cup or Trophy. The Plate was handcrafted by Flynn Silver, a family company from Kyneton in Victoria.

Due to scheduling issues, the second Nelson Mandela Challenge Plate match was incorporated into the Tri-Nations series (i.e. it was not an 'extra' match) and was played at Ellis Park Stadium in Johannesburg on 17 August 2002. It was Corné Krige's turn to raise the Plate after the Springboks scored late to win the thrilling match 33–31.

The Australian Rugby Union and the South African Rugby Union agreed for the Nelson Mandela Challenge Plate to be played within the Tri-Nations series as from 2006. Australia won the trophy in 2006 after beating South Africa 2–1 in the three tests they played. In 2007 Australia retained the Plate, as each team won one test in an abbreviated Tri-Nations because of the 2007 Rugby World Cup.

The complete list of Nelson Mandela Challenge Plate test matches is:

Date	Venue	Result	Holder
8 July 2000	Telstra Dome, Melbourne	AUS 44, SA 23	Australia
17 August 2002	Ellis Park, Johannesburg	SA 33, AUS 31	South Africa
9 July 2005	Telstra Stadium, Sydney	AUS 30, SA12	
23 July 2005	Ellis Park, Johannesburg	SA 33, AUS 20	South Africa

Date	Venue	Result	Holder
15 July 2006	Suncorp Stadium, Brisbane	AUS 49, SA 0	
5 August 2006	Telstra Stadium, Sydney	AUS 20, SA 18	Australia
9 September 2006	Ellis Park, Johannesburg	SA 24, AUS 16	
16 June 2007	Newlands, Cape Town	SA 22, AUS 19	
7 July 2007	Telstra Stadium, Sydney	AUS 25, SA 17	Australia
19 July 2008	Subiaco Oval, Perth	AUS 16, SA 9	
23 August 2008	Absa Stadium, Durban	SA 15, AUS 27	Australia
30 August 2008	Coca-Cola Park, Johannesburg	SA 53, AUS 8	
08 August 2009	Newlands, Cape Town	SA 29 AUS 17	
29 August 2009	Subiaco Oval, Perth	SA 32 AUS 25	
5 September 2009	Suncorp Stadium, Brisbane	SA 6 AUS 21	South Africa
24 July 2010	Suncorp Stadium, Brisbane	SA 13 AUS 30	
27 August 2010	Loftus Versfeld, Pretoria	SA 44 AUS 31	
4 September 2010	Vodacom Park, Bloemfontein	SA 39 AUS 41	Australia

— PRINCE WILLIAM CUP —

The Prince William Cup was created in 2007 by the Welsh Rugby Union, and celebrates 100 years of rugby union history between Wales and South Africa. It is named after the Vice Royal Patron of the WRU, Prince William, who presented the cup to the winners in the inaugural match held at the Millennium Stadium in Cardiff on Saturday 24 November 2007.

The specially commissioned Prince William Cup was designed by two of Wales's leading contemporary designer jewellers, Mari Thomas from Llanelli and Nicola Palterman from Neath. Prince William took a keen interest in the concept of the trophy and was personally involved in its design and the materials used. Made in silver, with a solid Welsh oak base, the maps of Wales and South Africa are etched onto the surface to create a stunning effect. The hammered edges spiralling around the trophy represent the landscape and mountains of Wales, while inscribed on it are some words of one of Nelson Mandela's most stirring quotes: 'The greatest glory in living lies not in never falling, but in rising every time we fall.'

The complete list of Prince William Cup matches is:

Date	Venue	Result	Holder
24 Nov 2007	Millenium Stadium, Cardiff	WAL 12, SA 34	South Africa
7 Jun 2008	Vodacom Park, Bloemfontein	SA 43, WAL 17	South Africa
14 Jun 2008	Loftus Versfeld, Pretoria	SA 37, WAL 21	South Africa
8 Nov 2008	Millenium Stadium, Cardiff	WAL 15, SA 20	South Africa
5 June 2010	Millennium Stadium, Cardiff	WAL 31 SA 34	South Africa
13 Nov 2010	Millennium Stadium, Cardiff	WAL 25 SA 29	South Africa

— GREAT REWARD —

Richard Prentis, loose-head prop of Diggers and Transvaal, played in 11 test matches in 1980 and 1981. He played in 4 further tour matches on the Springboks' tour to South America in 1980 where he was picked as lock in South Africa's first tour match against a Paraguay Invitation XV in Asunción. Prentis was also afforded the honour of captaining South Africa on that day, in what was to be his first and last match as Springbok captain. South Africa easily won 84–6.

— INSEPARABLE LOCKS —

Bakkies Botha and Victor Matfield have played together in 60 tests for South Africa. This is the world record for a lock pairing.

Botha and Matfield began their partnership against Scotland at Durban on 7 June 2003 on the occasion of Matfield's 14th cap and Botha's second, and since then South Africa have a test record 45 won and 15 lost with the two as partners in the second-row engine room.

Both received yellow cards against Scotland on 27 November 2004 at Edinburgh, Murrayfield, Botha in the 36th minute and Matfield in the 39th min. They sat in the sin-bin together for 7 playing minutes and the whole of half-time.

— SCORED TRIES AGAINST 16 OPPONENTS —

When Jaque Fourie scored his try against Italy In 2009, it meant that he had scored tries against all 16 different opponents he has played against, a unique feat in Springbok rugby. Just five players in world test rugby have scored tries against more different opponents: 20 – Daisuke Ohata (Japan); 16 – Marcello Cuttitta (Italy), David Campese (Australia), Brian O'Driscoll (Ireland) and Gareth Thomas (Wales).

— FIGHTING CAPTAINS —

In 1912 Billy Millar was involved in an incident at the final trials for the tour to the UK when he hit an opponent who, according to Millar, was looking for trouble during the whole of the game. The selectors decided not to appoint him as captain, but their decision was vetoed by the South African Rugby Board and he was duly appointed. In 1956 Salty du Rand was earmarked as captain of the Springboks' tour to Australasia. After the final trial, in which Jan Pickard's B side beat Du Rand's A side, Pickard made a remark about the game in the hotel where the players were staying. Du Rand didn't like the comment and hit Pickard. The selectors then changed their side and chose Basie Vivier as the captain. Ironically Du Rand captained the side against New Zealand on 14 July when Vivier was injured.

In 1975 at the final trials Morné du Plessis hit Kleintjie Grobler during the match. This case is very similar to the 1912 Billy Millar case. Millar and Du Plessis were both Western Province captains and as in 1912 the SA Rugby Board (led by Danie Craven) intervened and gave Du Plessis the captaincy.

— GOAL-KICKING FORWARDS —

These days, forwards who kick goals are a rarity. The last Springbok forward to score points from kicks was lock Tiny Naudé with a penalty goal against the British Lions at Cape Town on 13 July 1968.

The complete list is:

Name	Caps	C	PG	DG	GM	Goals	Career
Okey Geffin	7	9	10	-	-	19	1949–51
Tiny Naudé	14	4	11	-	-	15	1963–68
Dougie Morkel	9	7	5	-	-	12	1906–13
Barry Heatlie	6	3	-	-	-	3	1891–1903
Frik du Preez	38	1	2	-	-	3	1961–71
Hennie Muller	13	2	1	-	-	3	1949–53
Johan Claassen	28	2	-	-	-	2	1955–62
Phil Mostert	14	-	-	-	1	1	1921–32

— NUMBER NINE DROP —

Johannes 'Bolla' Conradie is the only scrumhalf to have scored a dropped goal for the Springboks in a test match. He did so in the 53rd minute of South Africa's 34–23 victory against Argentina at the Velez Sarsfield Stadium in Buenos Aires on 5 November 2005.

— CRADOCK'S TREBLE —

It is not commonly known that the Karoo town of Cradock produced three Springboks in 1949, namely Jorrie Jordaan, Fiks van der Merwe and Salty du Rand.

— NAKA – HAPPY IN FRONT OR BACK ROW —

Naka Drotské started playing hooker in 1993 after making his provincial debut for Free State in 1992 as a flank. He played his last game as a flank for Free State on 2 April 1993; on 5 June 1993 he played his first game as a hooker and on 13 November 1993 he made his Springbok debut as a hooker. Four of his 26 Springbok caps came as a replacement flank, the rest were at hooker.

— DAWIE FAST-TRACKED —

Dawie de Villiers made his test debut against the British Lions in the second test in 1962 after he made a remarkable recovery from injury. In the space of a month the 22-year-old scrumhalf earned Western Province, Junior Springbok and Springbok colours.

— FOLLOWING IN GRANDDAD'S FOOTSTEPS —

Marijke Nel, the oldest granddaughter of the legendary Springbok captain Philip 'Flip' Nel (16 caps, 1928–37), made history when she became a Springbok in 2006. The 38-year-old Nel made her debut against Netherlands as a fullback at the Absa Stadium in Durban on 24 June, kicking 5 conversions in a 135–0 victory, and went on to represent her country at the Women's Rugby World Cup in Edmonton, Canada, appearing in three games at fullback. Francois Louw, grandson of the former Springbok and Western Province stalwart, Jan Pickard made his Springbok debut in 2010 against Wales. He scored two tries in seven tests for his country.

— PRESIDENTS OF THE SA RUGBY UNION —

The idea of forming a South African Rugby Board was first discussed in 1888 when a team from Kimberley visited Cape Town. Mr Percy Ross-Frames of Kimberley was the first to take action, and he found a ready supporter in Mr William Bisset of Cape Town. As a result of their combined efforts it was decided to form a South African Rugby Board. Informally it was resolved that the president of the Board should be nominated by the centre where the next tournament was to be held, and it was agreed that Kimberley should be accorded the privilege of appointing the first president. Naturally, Mr Ross-Frames was elected first president of the Board that was established in 1889.

No	Name	Tenure
1	Percy Ross-Frames	27/08/1889 – 14/07/1893
2	'Billy' Simkins	14/07/1893 – 19/03/1913
3	William P Schreiner	19/03/1913 – 19/03/1915
4	'Jack' Heyneman	19/03/1915 – 30/03/1927

No	Name	Tenure
5	'Sport' Pienaar	30/03/1927 – 12/10/1953
6	Edgar Tudhope	26/02/1954 – 05/04/1956
7	Danie Craven	05/04/1956 – 23/03/1992
	Danie Craven[1]	23/03/1992 – 04/01/1993
8	Fritz Eloff	08/01/1993 – 12/03/1993
9	Ebrahim Patel[2]	23/03/1992 – 12/03/1993
	Ebrahim Patel[3]	12/03/1993 – 11/03/1994
	Fritz Eloff[2]	12/03/1993 – 11/03/1994
10	Louis Luyt	11/03/1994 – 12/05/1998
11	Silas Nkanunu[4]	29/05/1998 - 01/09/1998
	Silas Nkanunu	01/09/1998 – 05/12/2003
12	Brian van Rooyen	05/12/2003 – 24/02/2006
13	Oregan Hoskins	24/02/2006 – present date

[1] First Executive President after unification [2] Co-President [3] Executive President
[4] Acting President

— NICKNAMES —

The world of South African rugby has been enriched, perhaps more than any other country, by the use of colourful nicknames for its players. Here are some of the more unusual names which were used throughout the players' careers in preference to their given names:

'Tjol' Lategan
'Chum' Osche
'Buks' Marais
'Carrots' Geraghty
'Cowboy' Saunders
'Mannetjies' Roux
'Flappie' Lochner
'Biddy' Anderson
'Champion' Myburgh
'Mary' Jackson
'Popeye' Strydom
'Pally' Truter
'Uncle' Dobbin

'Mof' Myburgh
'Piston' van Wyk
'Hempies' du Toit
'Rampie' Stander
'Tank' van Rooyen
'Koei' Brink
'Klondyke' Raaff
'Saturday' Knight
'Bubbles' Koch
'Stompie' van der Merwe
'Tiny' Naudé
'Moaner' van Heerden
'Klippies' Kritzinger
'Kleintjie' Grobler
'Vleis' Visagie
'Jakkals' Keevy
'Ollie' le Roux
'Os' du Randt
'Bakkies' Botha
'Bolla' Conradie

— DATES PROVINCES WERE FOUNDED —

When the South African Rugby Board was formed in 1889, four provinces already existed, namely Western Province (formed in 1883), Griqualand West (1886), Eastern Province (1888) and Transvaal (1889). In 1889 the South African Rugby Board tournament was held in Kimberley and Western Province emerged as the winners. The following Unions were affiliated to the South African Rugby Board (now the South African Rugby Union) on the dates shown.

After South Africa's readmittance to international rugby in 1991, many of the provinces changed their names, hence the current names for those unions are also shown.

Province	Year	Current name
Western Province	1883	Western Province
Griqualand West	1886	Griquas
Eastern Province	1888	EP Kings
Transvaal	1889	Golden Lions

Province	Year	Current name
Natal	1890	Sharks
Border	1891	Border Bulldogs
Free State	1895	Free State Cheetahs
Rhodesia	1895	Zimbabwe
South Western Districts	1899	Eagles
North Eastern Districts	1903	*
South West Africa	1916	Namibia
Western Transvaal	1920	Leopards
Northern Transvaal	1938	Blue Bulls
Boland	1939	Boland Cavaliers
Eastern Transvaal	1947	Valke
North Western Cape	1966	*
North Eastern Cape	1966	*
Far North	1968	*
Northern Free State	1968	Griffons
Eastern Free State	1968	*
South Eastern Transvaal	1969	Mpumalanga Pumas
Stellaland	1973	*
Northern Natal	1973	*
Vaal Triangle	1982	*
Lowveld	1984	*

* Ceased to exist after 1995

The following teams also competed in competitions of the SARB:

SWD Federation	1978
Western Province League	1978
SA Rugby Association (East)	1978
SA Rugby Association (West)	1978
SA Rugby Association	1979
Winelands	1984
Transkei	1993

— TRI-NATIONS —

In 1995 the rugby administrators of Australia, New Zealand and South Africa formed SANZAR and approached Rupert Murdoch, the boss of News Corporation in Sydney, with a proposal to fund two new southern hemisphere competitions, the Super 12 and the Tri-Nations. Just after the Rugby World Cup in South Africa, Murdoch asked Sam Chisholm, the head of Murdoch's global television empire outside the USA, to contact Louis Luyt, who was appointed as chairman of SANZAR, and asked him to fly to London because he was ready to approve News Corporation's funding. The amount offered, which Luyt approved, was US$550 million for a decade of exclusive worldwide television and radio rights.

The first Tri-Nations tournament took place in 1996, with New Zealand and Australia kicking off the competition on 6 July 1996 at Athletic Park in Wellington, a game that New Zealand won comfortably by 43–6. The first two years were dominated by New Zealand who won the competition in 1996 and in 1997. In 1998 the Springboks won the title for the first time.

It is an interesting aside to note that no team has ever won the Tri-Nations and the Rugby World Cup in the same year.

Previous Winners:

1996 – New Zealand
1997 – New Zealand
1998 – South Africa
1999 – New Zealand
2000 – Australia
2001 – Australia
2002 – New Zealand
2003 – New Zealand
2004 – South Africa
2005 – New Zealand
2006 – New Zealand
2007 – New Zealand
2008 – New Zealand
2009 – South Africa
2010 – New Zealand

— FIRST TRIP TO FRANCE —

Paul Roos's team of 1906–07 were the first Springboks to cross the English Channel to play an unofficial match (on 3 January 1907 at the Parc des Princes) against a 'France' team drawn from the two Parisian clubs: Stade Francais and Racing Club de France. The official French team were in England at the time. The Springboks won 55–6 and scored 13 tries in the process. Dietlof Maré scored two trics and eight conversions for a personal total of 22 points.

— HALL OF FAME —

Nine former South African internationals have been inducted into the International Rugby Hall of Fame based in New Zealand. They are: Bennie Osler, Danie Craven, Hennie Muller, Frik du Preez, Morné du Plessis, Naas Botha, Danie Gerber, François Pienaar and Joost van der Westhuizen.

Dr Danie Craven, Barry Heatlie, Bennie Osler and Frik du Preez were also inducted into the IRB Hall of Fame.

— BROTHERLY AFFAIR —

The 1956 Springbok team to Australia and New Zealand was the first Springbok touring team not to include a pair of brothers. The sets of brothers on previous Springbok tours were: 1906–07 (Japie and Pietie le Roux; Dougie, Andrew and Sommie Morkel); 1912–13 (Richard, Freddie and John Luyt; Gerhard and Jackie Morkel); 1921 (Harry and Royal Morkel); 1931–32 (JC and Ponie van der Westhuizen; Boy and Fanie Louw); 1937 (Boy and Fanie Louw); 1951–52 (Stephen and Dennis Fry).

In 1961 the Wallabies undertook a short tour to South Africa for the first time. There were two brothers in the Wallaby team: John and Dick Thornett. Both were double internationals, representing Australia in rugby and water polo.

— SPRINGBOK LEGENDS: DANIE GERBER —

DANIE GERBER FACTFILE
Born: 14 April 1958 in Port Elizabeth, Eastern Cape
Provinces: Eastern Province, Free State, Western Province
Caps: 24 (W16, D0, L8)
Scoring: 19 tries, 1 conversion – 82 points
Springbok debut: 18 October 1980 vs South America (Wanderers Club, Montevideo)

Danie Gerber on his way to scoring another try for the Springboks.

Danie Gerber, the well-built centre from Despatch in the Eastern Cape, first made a name for himself in schoolboy rugby, representing Eastern Province at the annual Craven Week from 1975 to 1977 and playing for the SA Schools side in all those three years. He made his first-class debut for Eastern Province in 1978 and also played for Free State and Western Province during his career. He burst onto the international scene in 1980 in the Springbok tour to South America. Gerber was a nightmare for opposing sides in the eighties. Dr Danie Craven had the following to say about Gerber: 'Danie possesses unusual strength, speed and agility and using those skills and attributes he has scored tries other players would sell their soul for; one of the greatest centres ever to represent South Africa.' Gerber scored hat-tricks of tries against South America at Loftus Versfeld in 1982 and again against England at Ellis Park in 1984. He was also the South African Rugby Player of the Year in 1984. His 19 test tries was a South African record until James Small broke it against Scotland on 6 December 1997. Danie was also the South African record-holder of 158 tries in first class rugby from 1995 until this mark was broken by Chris Badenhorst in 1998. After he retired from first-class rugby, Gerber went into coaching and was assistant coach of the Pumas for many years.

— SPRINGBOK SKIPPERS —

John Smit, the Springbok World Cup winning captain in 2007, is the man who has led South Africa onto the field the most times as skipper. He has been captain of South Africa in 76 tests, which is a world record.

Here is a list of most captaincies for South Africa:

Captain	Tests as captain	Total tests	Debut as captain
John Smit	76	102	2003 vs Georgia
Gary Teichmann	36	42	1996 vs New Zealand
François Pienaar	29	9	1993 vs France
Dawie de Villiers	22	25	1965 vs New Zealand
Corné Krige	18	39	1999 vs Italy
André Vos	16	33	1999 vs Spain
Morné du Plessis	15	22	1975 vs France
Bob Skinstad	12	42	2001 vs Italy
Hannes Marais	11	35	1971 vs France
Avril Malan	10	16	1960 vs New Zealand
Joost van der Westhuizen	10	89	1999 vs New Zealand
Victor Matfield	15	105	2007 vs New Zealand

— CAPTAIN FANTASTIC —

Morné du Plessis, whose father Felix also captained the Springboks in 1949, is the Springbok captain who has the highest winning percentage in ten tests or more under his leadership. He only lost two tests in charge in his 15-match career as captain. The list is:

Percentage	Player	Matches	Won	Drawn	Lost
86,7%	Morné du Plessis	15	13	–	2
80,0%	Joost van der Westhuizen	10	8	–	2
72,2%	Gary Teichmann	36	26	–	10
67,1%	John Smit	76	51	1	24
66,7%	Victor Matfield	15	10	–	5
65,6%	François Pienaar	29	19	2	8
59,1%	Dawie de Villiers	22	13	4	5
56,3%	André Vos	16	9	–	7

Percentage	Player	Matches	Won	Drawn	Lost
55,6%	Hannes Marais	11	6	2	3
50,0%	Avril Malan	10	5	2	3
50,0%	Bob Skinstad	12	6	1	5

— FRONT ROWS FROM THE SAME PROVINCE —

There have been 25 occasions in the history of Springbok rugby that the whole front row were from one province. This occurred for the first time in 1933 against Australia in the second test when Paul Visser, Bert Kipling and Joe Nykamp of Transvaal anchored the scrum at Kingsmead in Durban.

The complete list is:

1933 vs Australia, 2nd test – Paul Visser, Bert Kipling, Joe Nykamp (Transvaal)
1958 vs France, 1st test – Chris Koch, Bertus van der Merwe and Piet du Toit (Boland)
1960 vs NZ, 2nd test – Chris Koch, Bertus van der Merwe and Piet du Toit (Boland)
1980 vs South America, 1st test – Richard Prentis, Dave Frederickson and Johan Strauss (Transvaal)
1981 vs New Zealand, 1st test – Henning van Aswegen, Robert Cockrell and Hempies du Toit (WP)
1999 vs. Spain, RWC – Ollie le Roux, Chris Rossouw and Adrian Garvey (KZN)
2000 vs. Canada – Rob Kempson, Charl Marais and Cobus Visagie (WP)
2000 vs. England, 2nd test – Rob Kempson, Charl Marais and Cobus Visagie (WP)
2000 vs. Australia, 1st test – Rob Kempson, Charl Marais and Cobus Visagie (WP)
2000 vs. New Zealand, 1st test – Rob Kempson, Charl Marais and Cobus Visagie (WP)
2000 vs. Australia, 2nd test – Rob Kempson, Charl Marais and Cobus Visagie (WP)
2000 vs. Australia, 3rd test – Rob Kempson, Charl Marais and Cobus Visagie (WP)
2007 vs England, 1st test – Deon Carstens, John Smit and BJ Botha (KZN)
2008 vs Wales, 2nd test – Tendai Mtawarira, John Smit and BJ Botha (KZN)

2008 vs Scotland – Tendai Mtawarira, Bismarck du Plessis and John Smit (KZN)
2008 vs England – Tendai Mtawarira, John Smit and Jannie du Plessis (KZN)
2009 Tendai Mtawarira, Bismarck du Plessis and John Smit (KZN) played together in seven test matches.
2010 Tendai Mtawarira, Bismarck du Plessis and Jannie du Plessis (KZN) played together in four test matches.

— HOOKERS FROM THE SAME PROVINCE —

On the 1956 tour to Australia and New Zealand, both hookers, Bertus van der Merwe and Melt Hanekom, were from Boland.

In 1980 against the touring British Lions, Willie Kahts was the hooker, with Ewoud Malan, also from Northern Transvaal, on the bench. In the 4th test Malan played when Kahts was unavailable due to injury.

In 1981 on the tour to New Zealand, Shaun Povey replaced the injured Willie Kahts during the tour. He was from Western Province, as was the other hooker in New Zealand, Robert Cockrell.

In 2007 John Smit was the hooker with Bismarck du Plessis, also from the Sharks, on the bench. Du Plessis also went to the Rugby World Cup in France as the second hooker in the squad.

In 2009 two of the three hookers in the team on the end-of-year tour, Chiliboy Ralepelle and Bandise Maku, were from the same province, the Blue Bulls.

— FROM THE SAME PROVINCE —

The two fullbacks on the 1931–32 tour to Great Britain, Gerry Brand and Jackie Tindall, were from the same province, Western Province, and also from the same club, Hamilton, which is something unique in Springbok history.

Both scrumhalves on the 1931–32 tour to Great Britain and to Australia, Pierre de Villiers and Danie Craven, were from Western Province. In 1937 they were also the two scrumhalves on the tour to Australia and New Zealand, but at that stage Craven played for Eastern Province.

— SUPER RUGBY FRANCHISES —

In the first two years of the Super 12 – in 1996 and 1997 – South Africa was represented by the best four provinces in the previous year's Currie Cup competition.

From 1998 South Africa entered four regional teams: Golden Cats (Free State, Golden Lions, Griquas and Griffons), Western Stormers (Western Province, SWD Eagles and Boland), Coastal Sharks (Sharks, Eastern Province and Border) and the Northern Bulls (Blue Bulls, Pumas, Falcons and Leopards).

In 1999 the Golden Cats became simply the Cats, Western Stormers shortened their name to just the Stormers, and the Coastal Sharks just the Sharks. In 2001 Northern Bulls changed to the Bulls.

In 2006 South Africa entered a fifth team when the competition was expanded to Super 14. The Cheetahs (consisting of the Free State, Griquas and the Griffons) became the extra team, the Cats changed the amalgamation to Golden Lions, Pumas and Leopards, whilst the Bulls combined the Blue Bulls and Falcons. The Stormers and the Sharks remained unchanged. In 2007 the Cats changed their name to the Lions.

— CURRIE CUP ORIGINS —

When the South African Rugby Board was formed in 1889, a tournament was held in Kimberley in the same year. The first official provincial game under the auspices of the SA Rugby Board took place on 28 August 1889 between Eastern Province and Western Province. Western Province won the tournament and received the Board Trophy. In 1891, when the first touring side from Great Britain visited South Africa, Sir Donald Currie, the founder of the Castle Line, gave them a cup for presentation to the team who gave the best performance against the visitors on tour. This cup was awarded to Griqualand West who lost only 0–3 (one try and one penalty) to Great Britain. At the time Currie made it quite clear that it was to be a floating trophy for an annual internal competition. The first Currie Cup tournament took place in Kimberley in 1892 with Western Province as the winners. Until 1920 the Currie Cup tournament was held at two venues: in 1914 at Durban and Pietermaritzburg, and in 1920 at Bloemfontein and Kimberley. After that teams played at their home venues. The first Currie Cup final took place in 1939 (prior to that the team on top of the log won the trophy). Originally the Currie Cup final did not take place every year, but since 1968 a final has been played each season. Western Province have won the most titles, namely 32 (including the win in 1899 when they received the Board trophy) with the Blue Bulls (formerly Northern Transvaal) in second place with 22 titles. Other teams to win the Currie Cup are: Golden Lions (9), the Sharks (5), Free State (4), Griqualand West (3) and Border (2).

— NEW SOUTH WALES OR AUSTRALIA? —

On 3 October 1986 the Council of the Australian Rugby Football Union retrospectively accorded full test match status on all the international matches New South Wales played whilst the Queensland Rugby Union ceased to operate between 1919 and 1929. The reason for this was that NSW, in the absence of rugby union in Queensland, were fielding the best sides that Australia could muster.

In 1921 South Africa had visited Australia and New Zealand for the first time. The Springboks played five matches in Australia, three against New South Wales, one against a Victorian XV and a game against a Metropolitan side. The Springboks won all five games comfortably before the New Zealand leg of the tour.

Due to the 1986 ruling these three games against NSW were now recognised as tests by Australia, but South Africa have never awarded test caps for those same games.

The only other occasion where the full South African side has played a touring fixture against a country who awarded caps was when the Springboks visited South America in 1980 and on 9 October beat Paraguay 84–6 in Asuncion.

— SPRINGBOK LEGENDS: JOEL STRANSKY —

Joel Theodore Stransky first caught the eye as a schoolboy when he played for the SA Schools side in 1984 when still in Grade 11, but for some strange reason he did not make the SA Schools side in 1985. Stransky made his provincial debut in 1987 for Northern Transvaal while still under 20, and his Natal debut a year later. In 1993 he made his international debut on the Springboks tour to Australia. Joel Stransky will always be remembered for ‘that dropped goal’ that won the Rugby World Cup in 1995.

JOEL STRANSKY FACTFILE
Born: 16 July 1967 in Pietermaritzburg, Natal
Provinces: Northern Transvaal, Natal, Western Province
Caps: 22 (W 16, D 0, L6)
Scoring: 240 points (6 tries, 30 conversions, 47 penalties and 3 dropped goals)
Springbok debut: vs Australia on 31 July 1993 in Sydney

Joel Stransky in action at the 1995 Rugby World Cup.

Stransky started the 1995 Rugby World Cup in style by scoring South Africa's first 'full house' (i.e. scoring in all four ways) against Australia in the opening match of the RWC at Newlands, Cape Town. He scored a try, a conversion, four penalties and a dropped goal that day at Newlands. On 24 June 1995 the Rugby World Cup final was decided at Ellis Park in Johannesburg between the two powerhouses of rugby, South Africa and New Zealand. After full time the scores were level at 9 points each. In extra time, New Zealand drew first blood by a penalty from Andrew Mehrtens. Joel answered with his third penalty of the day and the scores were level again (12 each). With less than five minutes to go, South Africa were awarded a scrum just inside the New Zealand 22 on the right side of the field. Joost van der Westhuizen fed Stransky with the ball and the gifted fly-half lofted a drop between the uprights. A few minutes later the final whistle went and everybody went berserk. No one was more overjoyed than President Nelson Mandela who, wearing a Springbok jersey with no. 6 on his back, had been introduced to the two teams before the start, and then had the honour of presenting François Pienaar with the coveted trophy. François Pienaar summed it up in his speech just after the game: 'Joel Stransky, you beaut.'

— COMBINATIONS —

Victor Matfield and Bakkies Botha hold the South African record for the most test matches as a combination with their 47 matches as the lock pairing.

Here is the list of the most tests for specific partnerships:

Front-row partners	
Os du Randt, John Smit and Eddie Andrews (2004–06)	14 Tests
Lock	
Victor Matfield and Bakkies Botha (2003–09)	60 Tests
Loose forward	
Gary Teichmann, André Venter and Rassie Erasmus (1997–99)	14 Tests
Ruben Kruger, Gary Teichmann and André Venter (1996–97)	14 Tests
Halfback	
Joost van der Westhuizen and Henry Honiball (1993–99)	24 Tests
C	
Jean de Villiers and Jaque Fourie (2005–10)	22 Tests
Back three	
Pieter Rossouw, Percy Montgomery and Stefan Terblanche	13 Tests

— BOSMAN, FROM NOWHERE TO SPRINGBOK —

Meyer Bosman, the Free State Cheetahs flyhalf and centre, had a meteoric rise in South African rugby. He started the 2005 season in the Free State under-21 side at flyhalf. He made his first of eight appearances for Free State on 5 August against the Griffons and made seven more appearances, starting only once against the Sharks on 8 October. In the Currie Cup final on 22 October he went on as a replacement and scored the winning try for Free State, their first Currie Cup title since 1976. On 19 November he made his Springbok debut against Wales at the Millennium Stadium just 106 days after his first-class debut, and at 20 years and 213 days was the fourth youngest Springbok since the Second World War.

— SOUTH AMERICA'S GREAT COMEBACK —

In 1982 a combined South American side visited South Africa for the second time. Players from Chile, Uruguay and Paraguay were included, but the bulk of the touring party were Argentinians. Two tests were scheduled – the first played on 27 March at Loftus Versfeld was won comfortably by South Africa 50–18. A week later, on 3 April at the Free

State Stadium in Bloemfontein, Hugo Porta's team sprang a great surprise and beat the Springboks 21–12 with Porta scoring all the points.

In 1991 Hugo Porta was appointed Argentine Ambassador to South Africa by President Carlos Menem, and in 1994 he became Argentina's Minister for Sport.

— SOUTH AFRICA'S TEST RESULTS 1891–2010 —

A complete list of the Springbok's 395 official test match results: South Africa's record in those matches is won 250, lost 126, drawn 19. They have scored 8 938 points from 1 113 tries, 715 conversions, 778 penalty goals, 93 dropped goals and one goal from a mark.

No	Date	Opponents	Tourny	Venue	Result
1	30 Jul 1891	Great Britain (1)		Port Elizabeth	Lost 0–4
2	29 Aug 1891	Great Britain (2)		Kimberley	Lost 0–3
3	5 Sep 1891	Great Britain (3)		Cape Town	Lost 0–4
4	30 Jul 1896	Great Britain (1)		Port Elizabeth	Lost 0–8
5	22 Aug 1896	Great Britain (2)		Johannesburg	Lost 8–17
6	29 Aug 1896	Great Britain (3)		Kimberley	Lost 3–9
7	5 Sep 1896	Great Britain (4)		Cape Town	Won 5–0
8	26 Aug 1903	Great Britain (1)		Johannesburg	Drawn 10–10
9	5 Sep 1903	Great Britain (2)		Kimberley	Drawn 0–0
10	12 Sep 1903	Great Britain (3)		Cape Town	Won 8–0
11	17 Nov 1906	Scotland		Glasgow	Lost 0–6
12	24 Nov 1906	Ireland		Belfast	Won 15–12
13	1 Dec 1906	Wales		Swansea	Won 11–0
14	8 Dec 1906	England		Crystal Palace	Drawn 3–3
15	6 Aug 1910	Great Britain (1)		Johannesburg	Won 14–10
16	27 Aug 1910	Great Britain (2)		Port Elizabeth	Lost 3–8
17	3 Sep 1910	Great Britain (3)		Cape Town	Won 21–5

RWC Rugby World Cup **TN** Tri-Nations **(1)** 1st Test **(2)** 2nd Test
(qf) Quarter-final **(sf)** Semi-final **(f)** Final **(3/4)** 3rd and 4th Place Playoff
(po) Play-off * After extra time

No	Date	Opponents	Tourny	Venue	Result
18	23 Nov 1912	Scotland		Inverleith	Won 16–0
19	30 Nov 1912	Ireland		Dublin	Won 38–0
20	14 Dec 1912	Wales		Cardiff	Won 3–0
21	4 Jan 1913	England		Twickenham	Won 9–3
22	11 Jan 1913	France		Bordeaux	Won 38–5
23	13 Aug 1921	New Zealand (1)		Dunedin	Lost 5–13
24	27 Aug 1921	New Zealand (2)		Auckland	Won 9–5
25	17 Sep 1921	New Zealand (3)		Wellington	Drawn 0–0
26	16 Aug 1924	Great Britain (1)		Durban	Won 7–3
27	23 Aug 1924	Great Britain (2)		Johannesburg	Won 17–0
28	13 Sep 1924	Great Britain (3)		Port Elizabeth	Drawn 3–3
29	20 Sep 1924	Great Britain (4)		Cape Town	Won 16–9
30	30 Jun 1928	New Zealand (1)		Durban	Won 17–0
31	21 Jul 1928	New Zealand (2)		Johannesburg	Lost 6–7
32	18 Aug 1928	New Zealand (3)		Port Elizabeth	Won 11–6
33	1 Sep 1928	New Zealand (4)		Cape Town	Lost 5–13
34	5 Dec 1931	Wales		Swansea	Won 8–3
35	19 Dec 1931	Ireland		Dublin	Won 8–3
36	2 Jan 1932	England		Twickenham	Won 7–0
37	16 Jan 1932	Scotland		Murrayfield	Won 6–3
38	8 Jul 1933	Australia (1)		Cape Town	Won 17–3
39	22 Jul 1933	Australia (2)		Durban	Lost 6–21
40	12 Aug 1933	Australia (3)		Johannesburg	Won 12–3
41	26 Aug 1933	Australia (4)		Port Elizabeth	Won 11–0
42	2 Sep 1933	Australia (5)		Bloemfontein	Lost 4–15
43	26 Jun 1937	Australia (1)		Sydney	Won 9–5
44	17 Jul 1937	Australia (2)		Sydney	Won 26–17
45	14 Aug 1937	New Zealand (1)		Wellington	Lost 7–13

RWC Rugby World Cup **TN** Tri-Nations **(1)** 1st Test **(2)** 2nd Test
(qf) Quarter-final **(sf)** Semi-final **(f)** Final **(3/4)** 3rd and 4th Place Playoff
(po) Play-off * After extra time

No	Date	Opponents	Tourny	Venue	Result
46	4 Sep 1937	New Zealand (2)		Christchurch	Won 13–6
47	25 Sep 1937	New Zealand (3)		Auckland	Won 17–6
48	6 Aug 1938	Great Britain (1)		Johannesburg	Won 26–12
49	3 Sep 1938	Great Britain (2)		Port Elizabeth	Won 19–3
50	10 Sep 1938	Great Britain (3)		Cape Town	Lost 16–21
51	16 Jul 1949	New Zealand (1)		Cape Town	Won 15–11
52	13 Aug 1949	New Zealand (2)		Johannesburg	Won 12–6
53	3 Sep 1949	New Zealand (3)		Durban	Won 9–3
54	17 Sep 1949	New Zealand (4)		Port Elizabeth	Won 11–8
55	24 Nov 1951	Scotland		Murrayfield	Won 44–0
56	8 Dec 1951	Ireland		Dublin	Won 17–5
57	22 Dec 1951	Wales		Cardiff	Won 6–3
58	5 Jan 1952	England		Twickenham	Won 8–3
59	16 Feb 1952	France		Paris	Won 25–3
60	22 Aug 1953	Australia (1)		Johannesburg	Won 25–3
61	5 Sep 1953	Australia (2)		Cape Town	Lost 14–18
62	19 Sep 1953	Australia (3)		Durban	Won 18–8
63	26 Sep 1953	Australia (4)		Port Elizabeth	Won 22–9
64	6 Aug 1955	British Isles (1)		Johannesburg	Lost 22–23
65	20 Aug 1955	British Isles (2)		Cape Town	Won 25–9
66	3 Sep 1955	British Isles (3)		Pretoria	Lost 6–9
67	24 Sep 1955	British Isles (4)		Port Elizabeth	Won 22–8
68	26 May 1956	Australia (1)		Sydney	Won 9–0
69	2 Jun 1956	Australia (2)		Brisbane	Won 9–0
70	14 Jul 1956	New Zealand (1)		Dunedin	Lost 6–10
71	4 Aug 1956	New Zealand (2)		Wellington	Won 8–3
72	18 Aug 1956	New Zealand (3)		Christchurch	Lost 10–17
73	1 Sep 1956	New Zealand (4)		Auckland	Lost 5–11

RWC Rugby World Cup **TN** Tri-Nations **(1)** 1st Test **(2)** 2nd Test
(qf) Quarter-final **(sf)** Semi-final **(f)** Final **(3/4)** 3rd and 4th Place Playoff
(po) Play-off * After extra time

No	Date	Opponents	Tourny	Venue	Result
74	26 Jul 1958	France (1)		Cape Town	Drawn 3–3
75	16 Aug 1958	France (2)		Johannesburg	Lost 5–9
76	30 Apr 1960	Scotland		Port Elizabeth	Won 18–10
77	25 Jun 1960	New Zealand (1)		Johannesburg	Won 13–0
78	23 Jul 1960	New Zealand (2)		Cape Town	Lost 3–11
79	13 Aug 1960	New Zealand (3)		Bloemfontein	Drawn 11–11
80	27 Aug 1960	New Zealand (4)		Port Elizabeth	Won 8–3
81	3 Dec 1960	Wales		Cardiff	Won 3–0
82	17 Dec 1960	Ireland		Dublin	Won 8–3
83	7 Jan 1961	England		Twickenham	Won 5–0
84	21 Jan 1961	Scotland		Murrayfield	Won 12–5
85	18 Feb 1961	France		Paris	Drawn 0–0
86	13 May 1961	Ireland		Cape Town	Won 24–8
87	5 Aug 1961	Australia (1)		Johannesburg	Won 28–3
88	12 Aug 1961	Australia (2)		Port Elizabeth	Won 23–11
89	23 Jun 1962	British Isles (1)		Johannesburg	Drawn 3–3
90	21 Jul 1962	British Isles (2)		Durban	Won 3–0
91	4 Aug 1962	British Isles (3)		Cape Town	Won 8–3
92	25 Aug 1962	British Isles (4)		Bloemfontein	Won 34–14
93	13 Jul 1963	Australia (1)		Pretoria	Won 14–3
94	10 Aug 1963	Australia (2)		Cape Town	Lost 5–9
95	24 Aug 1963	Australia (3)		Johannesburg	Lost 9–11
96	7 Sep 1963	Australia (4)		Port Elizabeth	Won 22–6
97	23 May 1964	Wales		Durban	Won 24–3
98	25 Jul 1964	France		Springs	Lost 6–8
99	10 Apr 1965	Ireland		Dublin	Lost 6–9
100	17 Apr 1965	Scotland		Murrayfield	Lost 5–8
101	19 Jun 1965	Australia (1)		Sydney	Lost 11–18

RWC Rugby World Cup **TN** Tri-Nations **(1)** 1st Test **(2)** 2nd Test
(qf) Quarter-final **(sf)** Semi-final **(f)** Final **(3/4)** 3rd and 4th Place Playoff
(po) Play-off * After extra time

No	Date	Opponents	Tourny	Venue	Result
102	26 Jun 1965	Australia (2)		Brisbane	Lost 8–12
103	31 Jul 1965	New Zealand (1)		Wellington	Lost 3–6
104	21 Aug 1965	New Zealand (2)		Dunedin	Lost 0–13
105	4 Sep 1965	New Zealand (3)		Christchurch	Won 19–16
106	18 Sep 1965	New Zealand (4)		Auckland	Lost 3–20
107	15 Jul 1967	France (1)		Durban	Won 26–3
108	22 Jul 1967	France (2)		Bloemfontein	Won 16–3
109	29 Jul 1967	France (3)		Johannesburg	Lost 14–19
110	12 Aug 1967	France (4)		Cape Town	Drawn 6–6
111	8 Jun 1968	British Isles (1)		Pretoria	Won 25–20
112	22 Jun 1968	British Isles (2)		Port Elizabeth	Drawn 6–6
113	13 Jul 1968	British Isles (3)		Cape Town	Won 11–6
114	27 Jul 1968	British Isles (4)		Johannesburg	Won 19–6
115	9 Nov 1968	France (1)		Bordeaux	Won 12–9
116	16 Nov 1968	France (2)		Paris	Won 16–11
117	2 Aug 1969	Australia (1)		Johannesburg	Won 30–11
118	16 Aug 1969	Australia (2)		Durban	Won 16–9
119	6 Sep 1969	Australia (3)		Cape Town	Won 11–3
120	20 Sep 1969	Australia (4)		Bloemfontein	Won 19–8
121	6 Dec 1969	Scotland		Murrayfield	Lost 3–6
122	20 Dec 1969	England		Twickenham	Lost 8–11
123	10 Jan 1970	Ireland		Dublin	Drawn 8–8
124	24 Jan 1970	Wales		Cardiff	Drawn 6–6
125	25 Jul 1970	New Zealand (1)		Pretoria	Won 17–6
126	8 Aug 1970	New Zealand (2)		Cape Town	Lost 8–9
127	29 Aug 1970	New Zealand (3)		Port Elizabeth	Won 14–3
128	12 Sep 1970	New Zealand (4)		Johannesburg	Won 20–17
129	12 Jun 1971	France (1)		Bloemfontein	Won 22–9

RWC Rugby World Cup **TN** Tri-Nations **(1)** 1st Test **(2)** 2nd Test
(qf) Quarter-final **(sf)** Semi-final **(f)** Final **(3/4)** 3rd and 4th Place Playoff
(po) Play-off * After extra time

No	Date	Opponents	Tourny	Venue	Result
130	19 Jun 1971	France (2)		Durban	Drawn 8–8
131	17 Jul 1971	Australia (1)		Sydney	Won 19–11
132	31 Jul 1971	Australia (2)		Brisbane	Won 14–6
133	7 Aug 1971	Australia (3)		Sydney	Won 18–6
134	3 Jun 1972	England		Johannesburg	Lost 9–18
135	8 Jun 1974	British Isles (1)		Cape Town	Lost 3–12
136	22 Jun 1974	British Isles (2)		Pretoria	Lost 9–28
137	13 Jul 1974	British Isles (3)		Port Elizabeth	Lost 9–26
138	27 Jul 1974	British Isles (4)		Johannesburg	Drawn 13–13
139	23 Nov 1974	France (1)		Toulouse	Won 13–4
140	30 Nov 1974	France (2)		Paris	Won 10–8
141	21 Jun 1975	France (1)		Bloemfontein	Won 38–25
142	28 Jun 1975	France (2)		Pretoria	Won 33–18
143	24 Jul 1976	New Zealand (1)		Durban	Won 16–7
144	14 Aug 1976	New Zealand (2)		Bloemfontein	Lost 9–15
145	4 Sep 1976	New Zealand (3)		Cape Town	Won 15–10
146	18 Sep 1976	New Zealand (4)		Johannesburg	Won 15–14
147	27 Aug 1977	World XV		Pretoria	Won 45–24
148	26 Apr 1980	South America (1)		Johannesburg	Won 24–9
149	3 May 1980	South America (2)		Durban	Won 18–9
150	31 May 1980	British Isles (1)		Cape Town	Won 26–22
151	14 Jun 1980	British Isles (2)		Bloemfontein	Won 26–19
152	28 Jun 1980	British Isles (3)		Port Elizabeth	Won 12–10
153	12 Jul 1980	British Isles (4)		Pretoria	Lost 13–17
154	18 Oct 1980	South America (1)		Montevideo	Won 22–13
155	25 Oct 1980	South America (2)		Santiago	Won 30–16
156	8 Nov 1980	France		Pretoria	Won 37–15
157	30 May 1981	Ireland (1)		Cape Town	Won 23–15

RWC Rugby World Cup **TN** Tri-Nations **(1)** 1st Test **(2)** 2nd Test
(qf) Quarter-final **(sf)** Semi-final **(f)** Final **(3/4)** 3rd and 4th Place Playoff
(po) Play-off * After extra time

No	Date	Opponents	Tourny	Venue	Result
158	6 Jun 1981	Ireland (2)		Durban	Won 12–10
159	15 Aug 1981	New Zealand (1)		Christchurch	Lost 9–14
160	29 Aug 1981	New Zealand (2)		Wellington	Won 24–12
161	12 Sep 1981	New Zealand (3)		Auckland	Lost 22–25
162	25 Sep 1981	United States		Glenville	Won 38–7
163	27 Mar 1982	South America (1)		Pretoria	Won 50–18
164	3 Apr 1982	South America (2)		Bloemfontein	Lost 12–21
165	2 Jun 1984	England (1)		Port Elizabeth	Won 33–15
166	9 Jun 1984	England (2)		Johannesburg	Won 35–9
167	20 Oct 1984	South America (1)		Pretoria	Won 32–15
168	27 Oct 1984	South America (2)		Cape Town	Won 22–13
169	10 May 1986	NZ Cavaliers (1)		Cape Town	Won 21–15
170	17 May 1986	NZ Cavaliers (2)		Durban	Lost 18–19
171	24 May 1986	NZ Cavaliers (3)		Pretoria	Won 33–18
172	31 May 1986	NZ Cavaliers (4)		Johannesburg	Won 24–10
173	26 Aug 1989	World XV (1)		Cape Town	Won 20–19
174	2 Sep 1989	World XV (2)		Johannesburg	Won 22–16
175	15 Aug 1992	New Zealand		Johannesburg	Lost 24–27
176	22 Aug 1992	Australia		Cape Town	Lost 3–26
177	17 Oct 1992	France (1)		Lyon	Won 20–15
178	24 Oct 1992	France (2)		Paris	Lost 16–29
179	14 Nov 1992	England		Twickenham	Lost 16–33
180	26 Jun 1993	France (1)		Durban	Drawn 20–20
181	3 Jul 1993	France (2)		Johannesburg	Lost 17–18
182	31 Jul 1993	Australia (1)		Sydney	Won 19–12
183	14 Aug 1993	Australia (2)		Brisbane	Lost 20–28
184	21 Aug 1993	Australia (3)		Sydney	Lost 12–19
185	6 Nov 1993	Argentina (1)		Buenos Aires	Won 29–26

RWC Rugby World Cup **TN** Tri-Nations **(1)** 1st Test **(2)** 2nd Test
(qf) Quarter-final **(sf)** Semi-final **(f)** Final **(3/4)** 3rd and 4th Place Playoff
(po) Play-off * After extra time

No	Date	Opponents	Tourny	Venue	Result
186	13 Nov 1993	Argentina (2)		Buenos Aires	Won 52–23
187	4 Jun 1994	England (1)		Pretoria	Lost 15–32
188	11 Jun 1994	England (2)		Cape Town	Won 27–9
189	9 Jul 1994	New Zealand (1)		Dunedin	Lost 14–22
190	23 Jul 1994	New Zealand (2)		Wellington	Lost 9–13
191	6 Aug 1994	New Zealand (3)		Auckland	Drawn 18–18
192	8 Oct 1994	Argentina (1)		Port Elizabeth	Won 42–22
193	15 Oct 1994	Argentina (2)		Johannesburg	Won 46–26
194	19 Nov 1994	Scotland		Murrayfield	Won 34–10
195	26 Nov 1994	Wales		Cardiff	Won 20–12
196	13 Apr 1995	Samoa		Johannesburg	Won 60–8
197	25 May 1995	Australia	RWC	Cape Town	Won 27–18
198	30 May 1995	Romania	RWC	Cape Town	Won 21–8
199	3 Jun 1995	Canada	RWC	Port Elizabeth	Won 20–0
200	10 Jun 1995	Samoa (qf)	RWC	Johannesburg	Won 42–14
201	17 Jun 1995	France (sf)	RWC	Durban	Won 19–15
202	24 Jun 1995	New Zealand (f)	RWC	Johannesburg	Won 15–12*
203	2 Sep 1995	Wales		Johannesburg	Won 40–11
204	12 Nov 1995	Italy		Rome	Won 40–21
205	18 Nov 1995	England		Twickenham	Won 24–14
206	2 Jul 1996	Fiji		Pretoria	Won 43–18
207	13 Jul 1996	Australia	TN	Sydney	Lost 16–21
208	20 Jul 1996	New Zealand	TN	Christchurch	Lost 11–15
209	3 Aug 1996	Australia	TN	Bloemfontein	Won 25–19
210	10 Aug 1996	New Zealand	TN	Cape Town	Lost 18–29
211	17 Aug 1996	New Zealand (1)		Durban	Lost 19–23
212	24 Aug 1996	New Zealand (2)		Pretoria	Lost 26–33
213	31 Aug 1996	New Zealand (3)		Johannesburg	Won 32–22

RWC Rugby World Cup **TN** Tri-Nations **(1)** 1st Test **(2)** 2nd Test
(qf) Quarter-final **(sf)** Semi-final **(f)** Final **(3/4)** 3rd and 4th Place Playoff
(po) Play-off * After extra time

No	Date	Opponents	Tourny	Venue	Result
214	9 Nov 1996	Argentina (1)		Buenos Aires	Won 46–15
215	16 Nov 1996	Argentina (2)		Buenos Aires	Won 44–21
216	30 Nov 1996	France (1)		Bordeaux	Won 22–12
217	7 Dec 1996	France (2)		Paris	Won 13–12
218	15 Dec 1996	Wales		Cardiff	Won 37–20
219	10 Jun 1997	Tonga		Cape Town	Won 74–10
220	21 Jun 1997	British Isles (1)		Cape Town	Lost 16–25
221	28 Jun 1997	British Isles (2)		Durban	Lost 15–18
222	5 Jul 1997	British Isles (3)		Johannesburg	Won 35–16
223	19 Jul 1997	New Zealand	TN	Johannesburg	Lost 32–35
224	2 Aug 1997	Australia	TN	Brisbane	Lost 20–32
225	9 Aug 1997	New Zealand	TN	Auckland	Lost 35–55
226	23 Aug 1997	Australia	TN	Pretoria	Won 61–22
227	8 Nov 1997	Italy		Bologna	Won 62–31
228	15 Nov 1997	France (1)		Lyon	Won 36–32
229	22 Nov 1997	France (2)		Paris	Won 52–10
230	29 Nov 1997	England		Twickenham	Won 29–11
231	6 Dec 1997	Scotland		Murrayfield	Won 68–10
232	13 Jun 1998	Ireland (1)		Bloemfontein	Won 37–13
233	20 Jun 1998	Ireland (2)		Pretoria	Won 33–0
234	27 Jun 1998	Wales		Pretoria	Won 96–13
235	4 Jul 1998	England		Cape Town	Won 18–0
236	18 Jul 1998	Australia	TN	Perth	Won 14–13
237	25 Jul 1998	New Zealand	TN	Wellington	Won 13–3
238	15 Aug 1998	New Zealand	TN	Durban	Won 24–23
239	22 Aug 1998	Australia	TN	Johannesburg	Won 29–15
240	14 Nov 1998	Wales		Wembley	Won 28–20
241	21 Nov 1998	Scotland		Murrayfield	Won 35–10

RWC Rugby World Cup **TN** Tri-Nations (1) 1st Test (2) 2nd Test
(qf) Quarter-final **(sf)** Semi-final **(f)** Final **(3/4)** 3rd and 4th Place Playoff
(po) Play-off * After extra time

No	Date	Opponents	Tourny	Venue	Result
242	28 Nov 1998	Ireland		Dublin	Won 27–13
243	5 Dec 1998	England		Twickenham	Lost 7–13
244	12 Jun 1999	Italy (1)		Port Elizabeth	Won 74–3
245	19 Jun 1999	Italy (2)		Durban	Won 101–0
246	26 Jun 1999	Wales		Cardiff	Lost 19–29
247	10 Jul 1999	New Zealand	TN	Dunedin	Lost 0–28
248	17 Jul 1999	Australia	TN	Brisbane	Lost 6–32
249	7 Aug 1999	New Zealand	TN	Pretoria	Lost 18–34
250	14 Aug 1999	Australia	TN	Cape Town	Won 10–9
251	3 Oct 1999	Scotland	RWC	Murrayfield	Won 46–29
252	10 Oct 1999	Spain	RWC	Murrayfield	Won 47–3
253	15 Oct 1999	Uruguay	RWC	Glasgow	Won 39–3
254	24 Oct 1999	England (qf)	RWC	Paris	Won 44–21
255	30 Oct 1999	Australia (sf)	RWC	Twickenham	Lost 21–27
256	4 Nov 1999	New Zealand (3/4) RWC	Cardiff	Won 22-18	
257	10 Jun 2000	Canada		East London	Won 51–18
258	17 Jun 2000	England (1)		Pretoria	Won 18–13
259	24 Jun 2000	England (2)		Bloemfontein	Lost 22–27
260	8 Jul 2000	Australia		Melbourne	Lost 23–44
261	22 Jul 2000	New Zealand	TN	Christchurch	Lost 12–25
262	29 Jul 2000	Australia	TN	Sydney	Lost 6–26
263	19 Aug 2000	New Zealand	TN	Johannesburg	Won 46–40
264	26 Aug 2000	Australia	TN	Durban	Lost 18–19
265	12 Nov 2000	Argentina		Buenos Aires	Won 37–33
266	19 Nov 2000	Ireland		Dublin	Won 28–18
267	26 Nov 2000	Wales		Cardiff	Won 23–13
268	2 Dec 2000	England		Twickenham	Lost 17–25

RWC Rugby World Cup **TN** Tri-Nations **(1)** 1st Test **(2)** 2nd Test
(qf) Quarter-final **(sf)** Semi-final **(f)** Final **(3/4)** 3rd and 4th Place Playoff
(po) Play-off * After extra time

No	Date	Opponents	Tourny	Venue	Result
269	16 Jun 2001	France (1)		Johannesburg	Lost 23–32
270	23 Jun 2001	France (2)		Durban	Won 20–15
271	30 Jun 2001	Italy		Port Elizabeth	Won 60–14
272	21 Jul 2001	New Zealand	TN	Cape Town	Lost 3–12
273	28 Jul 2001	Australia	TN	Pretoria	Won 20–15
274	18 Aug 2001	Australia	TN	Perth	Drawn14–14
275	25 Aug 2001	New Zealand	TN	Auckland	Lost 15–26
276	10 Nov 2001	France		Paris	Lost 10–20
277	17 Nov 2001	Italy		Genova	Won 54–26
278	24 Nov 2001	England		Twickenham	Lost 9–29
279	1 Dec 2001	United States		Houston	Won 43–20
280	8 Jun 2002	Wales (1)		Bloemfontein	Won 34–19
281	15 Jun 2002	Wales (2)		Cape Town	Won 19–8
282	29 Jun 2002	Argentina		Springs	Won 49–29
283	6 Jul 2002	Samoa		Pretoria	Won 60–18
284	20 Jul 2002	New Zealand	TN	Wellington	Lost 20–41
285	27 Jul 2002	Australia	TN	Brisbane	Lost 27–38
286	10 Aug 2002	New Zealand	TN	Durban	Lost 23–30
287	17 Aug 2002	Australia	TN	Johannesburg	Won 33–31
288	9 Nov 2002	France		Marseille	Lost 10–30
289	16 Nov 2002	Scotland		Murrayfield	Lost 6–21
290	23 Nov 2002	England		Twickenham	Lost 3–53
291	7 Jun 2003	Scotland (1)		Durban	Won 29–25
292	14 Jun 2003	Scotland (2)		Johannesburg	Won 28–19
293	28 Jun 2003	Argentina		Port Elizabeth	Won 26–25
294	12 Jul 2003	Australia	TN	Cape Town	Won 26–22
295	19 Jul 2003	New Zealand	TN	Pretoria	Lost 16–52
296	2 Aug 2003	Australia	TN	Brisbane	Lost 9–29

RWC Rugby World Cup **TN** Tri-Nations **(1)** 1st Test **(2)** 2nd Test
(qf) Quarter-final **(sf)** Semi-final **(f)** Final **(3/4)** 3rd and 4th Place Playoff
(po) Play-off * After extra time

No	Date	Opponents	Tourny	Venue	Result
297	9 Aug 2003	New Zealand	TN	Dunedin	Lost 11–19
298	11 Oct 2003	Uruguay	RWC	Perth	Won 72–6
299	18 Oct 2003	England	RWC	Perth	Lost 6–25
300	24 Oct 2003	Georgia	RWC	Sydney	Won 46–19
301	1 Nov 2003	Samoa	RWC	Brisbane	Won 60–10
302	8 Nov 2003	New Zealand (qf)	RWC	Melbourne	Lost 9–29
303	12 Jun 2004	Ireland (1)		Bloemfontein	Won 31–17
304	19 Jun 2004	Ireland (2)		Cape Town	Won 26–17
305	26 Jun 2004	Wales		Pretoria	Won 53–18
306	17 Jul 2004	Pacific Islanders		Gosford	Won 38–24
307	24 Jul 2004	New Zealand	TN	Christchurch	Lost 21–23
308	31 Jul 2004	Australia	TN	Perth	Lost 26–30
309	14 Aug 2004	New Zealand	TN	Johannesburg	Won 40–26
310	21 Aug 2004	Australia	TN	Durban	Won 23–19
311	6 Nov 2004	Wales		Cardiff	Won 38–36
312	13 Nov 2004	Ireland		Dublin	Lost 12–17
313	20 Nov 2004	England		Twickenham	Lost 16–32
314	27 Nov 2004	Scotland		Murrayfield	Won 45–10
315	4 Dec 2004	Argentina		Buenos Aires	Won 39–7
316	11 Jun 2005	Uruguay		East London	Won 134–3
317	18 Jun 2005	France (1)		Durban	Drawn 30–30
318	25 Jun 2005	France (2)		Port Elizabeth	Won 27–13
319	9 Jul 2005	Australia		Sydney	Lost 12–30
320	23 Jul 2005	Australia		Johannesburg	Won 33–20
321	30 Jul 2005	Australia	TN	Pretoria	Won 22–16
322	6 Aug 2005	New Zealand	TN	Cape Town	Won 22–16
323	20 Aug 2005	Australia	TN	Perth	Won 22–19
324	27 Aug 2005	New Zealand	TN	Dunedin	Lost 27–31

RWC Rugby World Cup **TN** Tri-Nations **(1)** 1st Test **(2)** 2nd Test
(qf) Quarter-final **(sf)** Semi-final **(f)** Final **(3/4)** 3rd and 4th Place Playoff
(po) Play-off * After extra time

No	Date	Opponents	Tourny	Venue	Result
325	5 Nov 2005	Argentina		Buenos Aires	Won 34–23
326	19 Nov 2005	Wales		Cardiff	Won 33–16
327	26 Nov 2005	France		Paris	Lost 20–26
328	10 Jun 2006	Scotland (1)		Durban	Won 36–16
329	17 Jun 2006	Scotland (2)		Port Elizabeth	Won 29–15
330	24 Jun 2006	France		Cape Town	Lost 26–36
331	15 Jul 2006	Australia	TN	Brisbane	Lost 0–49
332	22 Jul 2006	New Zealand	TN	Wellington	Lost 17–35
333	5 Aug 2006	Australia	TN	Sydney	Lost 18–20
334	26 Aug 2006	New Zealand	TN	Pretoria	Lost 26–45
335	2 Sep 2006	New Zealand	TN	Rustenburg	Won 21–20
336	9 Sep 2006	Australia	TN	Johannesburg	Won 24–16
337	11 Nov 2006	Ireland		Dublin	Lost 15–32
338	18 Nov 2006	England (1)		Twickenham	Lost 21–23
339	25 Nov 2006	England (2)		Twickenham	Won 25–14
340	26 May 2007	England (1)		Bloemfontein	Won 58–10
341	2 Jun 2007	England (2)		Pretoria	Won 55–22
342	9 Jun 2007	Samoa		Johannesburg	Won 35–8
343	16 Jun 2007	Australia	TN	Cape Town	Won 22–19
344	23 Jun 2007	New Zealand	TN	Durban	Lost 21–26
345	7 Jul 2007	Australia	TN	Sydney	Lost 17–25
346	14 Jul 2007	New Zealand	TN	Christchurch	Lost 6–33
347	15 Aug 2007	Namibia		Cape Town	Won 105–13
348	25 Aug 2007	Scotland		Murrayfield	Won 27–3
349	9 Sep 2007	Samoa	RWC	Paris	Won 59–7
350	14 Sep 2007	England	RWC	Paris	Won 36–0
351	22 Sep 2007	Tonga	RWC	Lens	Won 30–25
352	30 Sep 2007	United States	RWC	Montpellier	Won 64–15

RWC Rugby World Cup **TN** Tri-Nations **(1)** 1st Test **(2)** 2nd Test
(qf) Quarter-final **(sf)** Semi-final **(f)** Final **(3/4)** 3rd and 4th Place Playoff
(po) Play-off * After extra time

No	Date	Opponents	Tourny	Venue	Result
353	7 Oct 2007	Fiji (qf)	RWC	Marseille	Won 37–20
354	14 Oct 2007	Argentina (sf)	RWC	Paris	Won 37–13
355	20 Oct 2007	England (f)	RWC	Paris	Won 15–6
356	24 Nov 2007	Wales		Cardiff	Won 34–12
357	7 Jun 2008	Wales (1)		Bloemfontein	Won 43–17
358	14 Jun 2008	Wales (2)		Pretoria	Won 37–21
359	21 Jun 2008	Italy		Cape Town	Won 26–0
360	5 Jul 2008	New Zealand	TN	Wellington	Lost 8–19
361	12 Jul 2008	New Zealand	TN	Dunedin	Won 30–28
362	19 Jul 2008	Australia	TN	Perth	Lost 9–16
363	9 Aug 2008	Argentina		Johannesburg	Won 63–9
364	16 Aug 2008	New Zealand	TN	Cape Town	Lost 0–19
365	23 Aug 2008	Australia	TN	Durban	Lost 15–27
366	30 Aug 2008	Australia	TN	Johannesburg	Won 53–8
367	8 Nov 2008	Wales		Cardiff	Won 20–15
368	15 Nov 2008	Scotland		Murrayfield	Won 14–10
369	22 Nov 2008	England		Twickenham	Won 42–6
370	20 Jun 2009	British and Irish Lions		Durban	Won 26–21
371	27 Jun 2009	British and Irish Lions		Pretoria	Won 28–25
372	4 Jul 2009	British and Irish Lions		Johannesburg	Lost 9–28
373	25 Jul 2009	New Zealand	TN	Bloemfontein	Won 28–9
374	1 Aug 2009	New Zealand	TN	Durban	Won 31–19
375	8 Aug 2009	Australia	TN	Cape Town	Won 29–17
376	29 Aug 2009	Australia	TN	Perth	Won 32–25
377	5 Sep 2009	Australia	TN	Brisbane	Lost 6–21

RWC Rugby World Cup **TN** Tri-Nations **(1)** 1st Test **(2)** 2nd Test
(qf) Quarter-final **(sf)** Semi-final **(f)** Final **(3/4)** 3rd and 4th Place Playoff
(po) Play-off * After extra time

No	Date	Opponents	Tourny	Venue	Result
378	12 Sep 2009	New Zealand	TN	Hamilton	Won 32–29
379	13 Nov 2009	France		Toulouse	Lost 13–20
380	21 Nov 2009	Italy		Florence	Won 32–10
381	28 Nov 2009	Ireland		Dublin	Lost 10–15
382	5 June 2010	Wales		Cardiff	Won 34–31
383	12 June 2010	France		Cape Town	Won 42–17
384	19 June 2010	Italy		Witbank	Won 29–13
385	26 June 2010	Italy		East London	Won 55–11
386	10 Jul 2010	New Zealand	TN	Auckland	Lost 12–32
387	17 Jul 2010	New Zealand	TN	Wellington	Lost 17–31
388	24 Jul 2010	Australia	TN	Brisbane	Lost 13–30
389	21 Aug 2010	New Zealand	TN	Soweto	Lost 22–29
390	28 Aug 2010	Australia	TN	Pretoria	Won 44–31
391	4 Sep 2010	Australia	TN	Bloemfontein	Lost 39–41
392	6 Nov 2010	Ireland		Dublin	Won 23–21
393	13 Nov 2010	Wales		Cardiff	Won 29–25
394	20 Nov 2010	Scotland		Edinburgh	Lost 17–21
395	27 Nov 2010	England		London	Won 21–11

RWC Rugby World Cup **TN** Tri-Nations **(1)** 1st Test **(2)** 2nd Test
(qf) Quarter-final **(sf)** Semi-final **(f)** Final **(3/4)** 3rd and 4th Place Playoff
(po) Play-off * After extra time

— BIBLIOGRAPHY —

The following books were consulted in compiling *The Springbok Handbook:*

Colquhoun, Andy (Ed): *SA Rugby Annual* (several editions)
Craven, Danie and Piet Jordaan: *Met die Maties op die Rugbyveld 1880–1955* (1955)
Craven, Danie: *Springbok Story 1949–1953* (1954)
Craven, DH: *Springbok Annals 1891–1958* (1964)
Difford, Ivor D: *History of South African Rugby Football* (1933)
Dobson, Paul: *Rugby in South Africa – A History 1861–1988* (1989)
Greyvenstein, Chris: *Springbok Saga* (1977)
Greyvenstein, Chris: *Springbok Rugby – An Illustrated History* (1995)
Greyvenstein, Chris: *They Made Headlines* (1972)
Griffiths, John: *The Phoenix Book of International Rugby Records* (1987)
Heath, Duane & Grieb, Eddie (Ed): *SA Rugby Annual* (2009–2011 editions)
Howitt, Bob: *SANZAR Saga* (2005)
Le Roux, Herman: *Sportpourri* (1998)
Mulford, John G: *Guardians of the Game* (2005)
Parker, AC: *W.P. Rugby Centenary 1883–1983* (1983)
Retief, Dan (Ed) *SA & Overseas Rugby,* July 1981 edition.
Rugby magazine: Vol 1 No 1 – Vol 2 No 12, Apr 1974 – Mar 1976
Shnaps, Teddy: *A Statistical History of Springbok Rugby* (1989)
Smit, Kobus: *The complete book of Springbok Rugby Records* (2007)
Van Rensburg, Frikkie: *G.W. Rugby 'n Honderd jaar 1886–1986* (1986)
Van Rooyen, Quintus (Ed): *SA Rugby Annual* (several editions)
Van Zyl, Hans and Piet van der Schyff: *Mielieboersage Wes-Transvaal Rugby 75* (1920–1975)

— PRIVATE MUSEUMS —

Derek Roos' Springbok jersey collection
Heinrich Schulze's private rugby museum